Toward High-quality Education in Peru

Standards, Accountability, and Capacity Building

THE WORLD BANK
Washington, D.C.

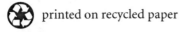
1 2 3 4 5 10 09 08 07

World Bank Country Studies are among the many reports originally prepared for internal use as part of the continuing analysis by the Bank of the economic and related conditions of its developing member countries and to facilitate its dialogs with the governments. Some of the reports are published in this series with the least possible delay for the use of governments, and the academic, business, financial, and development communities. The manuscript of this paper therefore has not been prepared in accordance with the procedures appropriate to formally-edited texts. Some sources cited in this paper may be informal documents that are not readily available.

ISBN-10: 0-8213-7017-0   ISBN-13: 978-0-8213-7017-9
eISBN: 978-0-8213-7018-6
ISSN: 0253-2123   DOI: 10.1596/978-0-8213-7017-9

Library of Congress Cataloging-in-Publication.

Toward high-quality education in Peru : standards, accountability, and
capacity building.
     p. cm. — (A World Bank country study)
   Includes bibliographical references.
   ISBN-13: 978-0-8213-7017-9
   ISBN-10: 0-8213-7017-0
   ISBN-13: 978-0-8213-7018-6 (electronic)
  1. Education—Peru. 2. Educational indicators—Peru. I. World Bank.
  LA596.T69 2007
  370.985—dc22
                                        2007015903

Contents

Foreword.. vii

Acknowledgments ix

Acronyms and Abbreviations xi

Executive Summary.. xiii

1. Overview of Current Indicators 1
   Coverage... 1
   Learning and Quality... 3

2. Educational Diagnostics and Recommendations 9
   Stock of Peruvian Research on "What Works" in Schooling 9
   Existing Stock of Policy Suggestions 17
   Remaining Impediments....................................... 21

3. The Accountability-Triangle Approach 23

4. Education Finance 25
   Patterns of Educational Expenditure......................... 25
   Education System Efficiency................................. 28
   Spending Incidence and Equity 35
   Distribution of Results 43
   Summary of Inequality of Benefits 52
   Special Focus on Teacher Costs 53
   Other Input Supplies.. 58

5. Why Don't Some Peruvian Children Finish High School? 61
   The Quantitative Evidence 62
   Returns to Education.. 65
   Qualitative Analysis of Dropout Motivations 68
   Policy Implications 70

6. Reading in the Early Grades: A Case Study in the Use of Standards 73
   Simple Reading Benchmarks 74
   Aims, Method, and Sample.................................... 76
   Basic Results... 77
   Some Causal Analysis Related to Standards and Support 83

 7. **School Management Issues**...89

  Behavior and Choice in Peru's Public Schools 89

  Direct Relationship Between Schools and Community: *Fe y Alegría*
  and the "Directed Autonomy" Model 100

 8. **Progress and Paralysis on Intercultural and Bilingual Education:
    A Special Problem with Standards** 111

  The Issue..111

  What Does it Take, and Is Peru Doing What it Takes? 113

  A Special Issue Related to "Compact" and Accountability:
  Standards and Standardization in EIB.....................................117

 9. **Participation and Decentralization: Little Effect, Some Potential** 121

  School Level 122

  Levels Above the School 123

  A Way Forward on Voice and Participation? Opportunities
  and Dangers in Decentralization 125

10. **Policy Recommendations** 129

  Standards 129

  Accountability 131

  Support...132

Appendixes

  A. Dogo 135

  B. Classification and Frequency of Classroom Activities....................137

Bibliography...141

LIST OF TABLES

1.1. Education System Coverage Data for Peru and Latin America as a Whole........2

2.1. Factors Associated with Improved Learning Results in Peru 12

2.2. Results on Determinants of Learning Based on 2001 National Evaluation 15

2.3. Results on Determinants of Learning Based on 2001 National Evaluation 16

2.4. Summary of Policy Recommendations in Some Key Peruvian
     Literature and Literature on Peru......................................18

4.1. Calculation of Expenditure Benchmarks Suitable for Peru 26

4.2. Key Expenditure Patterns in Peru......................................30

4.3. Beneficiary Incidence by Quintile, 2003 (assuming *equal*
     spending per beneficiary) 36

4.4. Benefit Incidence by Quintile, 2003 (assuming *unequal*
     spending per beneficiary) 36

4.5. Benefit or Beneficiary Incidence—International Medians in Various Years 36

4.6. Demographic and Public Private Choice of Families, by Income Quintile, as Determinants of Pro-poor Spending, 2003 37

4.7. Proportion of Youths Enrolled in School 2003 38

4.8. Benefits Represented by Public School Subsidy as a Proportion of Total Household Expenditure Across All Households ("Relative Incidence"), 2003 39

4.9. Per Student Spending and Poverty Levels by Region, 2003 40

4.10. Summary on Inequality of Various Educational Benefits. 52

4.11. Pupil-Teacher Ratios in Peru and Average for Latin America 55

4.12. Teacher Salaries in Peru, 1999–2004. 55

4.13. Textbook Provision in Peru: Selected Data 59

5.1. Quantitative Evidence on Dropping Out of School 63

5.2. Public and Private Returns to Education. 68

6.1. Basic Sample Characteristics for School Reading Standards Survey 78

6.2. Basic Results 78

6.3. School-level Reading Factor Correlations 79

6.4. Relationship Between Reading and Comprehension 80

6.5. School-by-School and Type-by-Type Variation in Reading Ability. 81

6.6. Reported Week of Textbook Arrival in the Classroom 86

6.7. Teacher Use of Classroom Time 86

7.1. Schools Chosen for Assessing School Effectiveness Factors 92

7.2. Tallies of Effectiveness Factors 95

7.3. Official and *Fe y Alegría* Curricular Statements Compared 104

8.1. Tasks or Requirements Needed to Successfully Implement EIB and Degree of Presence in Peru 113

8.2. Projects in Educación Intercultural Bilingüe in Peru 116

LIST OF FIGURES

1.1. Real and Predicted PISA Scores. 3

1.2. Relationship Between Access and Learning Scores 4

1.3. Frequency Distribution PISA 2000 Reading Performance 5

1.4. Cumulative Frequency PISA 2000 Reading Performance. 6

1.5. Economic versus Educational Inequality. 7

3.1. Accountability Triangle 24

4.1. Impact of Spending on Enrollment 29

4.2. Learning Efficiency of Peru's Education Expenditure. 33

4.3. Efficiency Frontier for Primary Education. 33

4.4. Efficiency Frontier for Secondary Education. 34

4.5. Correlation Between Poverty and Spending Across Regions 41

4.6. Socioeconomic Index and Spanish Performance Across Schools 44

4.7. Socioeconomic Index and Mother Tongue Across Schools 45

4.8. Variation of Results Among the Poor versus the Less Poor, Controlling for Language 46

4.9. Nutritional Variability Among the Poor and Non-poor. 47

4.10. Infrastructure, Supplies, and Learning Results 48

4.11. Socioeconomic Index and Quality of Input Supply 49

4.12. Socioeconomic Index and Infrastructure Supply 50

4.13. Learning Results and Pupil-Teacher Ratio. 51

4.14. Learning Results Residuals and Pupil-Teacher Ratio 52

4.15. Socioeconomic Index and School Supplies 59

4.16. School Supplies and Learning. 60

5.1. Age and School Enrollment by Income Group 64

5.2. Age and School Enrollment by Place of Residence 64

5.3. Age and School Enrollment by Gender 65

5.4. Grade-specific Enrollment Ratios by Place of Residence 66

5.5. Grade-specific Enrollment Ratios: Impact of Repetition 66

5.6. Grade-specific Enrollment Ratios by Gender 67

5.7. Returns to Education in Peru 67

5.8. Returns to Education Around the World. 68

Foreword

One of the principal challenges in reducing poverty and accelerating development in Peru is improving the quality of education. This book is a contribution from the World Bank to the debate over how to improve the quality of education. The country has had major successes in education coverage at all levels, reaching higher levels than in neighboring countries and higher in comparison to some countries with higher income levels. However, every measure of quality has shown there is a large gap between the impressive achievements in coverage and the little achieved in quality.

The book offers a diagnostic on the state of basic education in Peru and identifies the principal measures necessary to overcome the current stagnation in quality. It analyzes the state of education in Peru based on international comparisons, with both Latin American and other developing countries. The analysis includes a review of statistics on coverage, quality and inequality as well as a careful analysis of public spending on education, examining the amount spent and how it is distributed and re-examining some familiar places in a new light. Peruvian specialists have done many good studies in recent years and these are compared with each other and with the results of this book's analysis to identify areas of consensus as well as the value added from this study. The book also includes an analysis of less studied themes including a search for lessons learned in poor areas of Peru. This analysis includes a review of the administration system of the *Fe y Alegria* school system and a study of the administration patterns of well-regarded public schools. Finally, the book includes a study on the difficulties of bilingual education that are specific to Peru.

The book has three main recommendations that, to be successful, should be implemented sequentially. First, it is necessary to generate basic standards, quality goals, and quality measurement systems. Second, once quality can be measured a clear system of accountability should be implemented based on these standards and quality goals. The clients will play a central role in these systems by demanding their rights to quality services; this will only become possible once there are standards and goals that clarify clients' rights. Third, once there are standards and systems of accountability, investment is needed to strengthen the institutional capacity of the providers. This investment will have to cover different areas, and include training directly linked to pedagogical needs.

The book has been prepared by a team of World Bank officers and Peruvian consultants. Luis Crouch led the team and was the principal author of this book. This book is one product in a multisectoral analysis financed by the World Bank and the UK government's Department for International Development (DFID). The project, known as RECURSO, (which in Spanish stands for Bringing Accountability to Social Reform in Peru), was made up of six teams that worked together in a conceptual framework that emphasized accountability. The RECURSO project has presented its conclusions in various formats aimed at different audiences, which are available to interested parties at www.bancomundial.org.pe/NuevoContratoSocial, and include:

- A summary,
- Two videos aimed at parents and community leaders,

■ A series of short radio programs in Spanish, Quechua, Aymará, and Asháninka,
■ Various simplified pamphlets (on education, health, social assistance, and social participation), and
■ Various technical documents for reference.

Daniel Cotlear
Sector Manager for Education, Health and Social Protection
Bolivia, Ecuador, Perú and Venezuela
Latin America and the Caribbean
The World Bank

Acknowledgments

This document is the result of collaboration between the principal author, Luis Crouch, and the authors of the supporting studies, as well as other professionals. However, the final conclusions and any errors are the responsibility of the principal author. Lorena Alcázar and Néstor Valdivia of GRADE provided the research and analysis on *Fe y Alegría,* effective schools, and school-leaving problems. Marcela Echegaray, Consuelo Pasco and Jessyca Sampe from TAREA provided the research and analysis on reading and the use of standards in the early grades of Peruvian education. Lilliam Hidalgo Collazos and Ingrid Guzmán Sota from TAREA carried out the research and provided the commentary on Intercultural Bilingual Education. Flavio Figallo from the Pontificia Universidad Católica del Perú contributed the analysis of civil society participation. Pablo Lavado played a leading role in most of the numerical analysis and was the principal author of some sections such as the one on rates of return on education. Helen Abadzi of the World Bank provided valuable comments and text on reading standards. Finally, all the members of the RECURSO team, led by Daniel Cotlear, contributed valuable feedback, opportunities for professional debate and mutual enrichment during the many hours of team meetings.

The study benefited from the revision and incisive commentaries of World Bank colleagues including Bárbara Bruns, Ernesto Cuadra, Bob Prouty, and Kin Bing Wu (peer reviewers), and Ariel Fiszbein and Eduardo Velez; as well as World Bank personnel and consultants in Lima including John Newman, Betty M. Alvarado, Livia M. Benavides, Luisa Yesquén, Sandra Arzubiaga, and Carmen Osorio.

Barbara Hunt, who has been observing the Peruvian education sector for a long time, contributed valuable comments as part of the external review.

Peruvian intellectuals, technicians, and political leaders whose feedback, support or challenges made this a better product and whose comments were extremely valuable in shaping our perceptions included Santiago Cueto, Juan Fernando Vega, Nicolás Lynch, Manuel Bello, Manuel Iguíñiz, Sigfredo Chiroque, Martín Vegas, Patricia Salas O'Brien, Gloria Helfer, Mercedes Cabanillas, and Richard Webb. The technical teams for education of several Peruvian political parties shared their ideas with us during the policy dialogue—we recognize and thank them for their time and interest.

Among other donor agencies, support and feedback were received from Mark Lewis (DFID), Fernando Bolaños (USAID) and Antonieta de Harwood (USAID/AED, Head of the AprenDes project), among others.

In the government we extend our gratitude to all who contributed data, gave their time for interviews, and facilitated the process including Education Minister Javier Sota Nadal and the Vice Education Minister Idel Vexler, as well as Gustavo Cabrera, Giuliana Espinosa, Flormarina Guardia, Liliana Miranda, Luis Paz, Enrique Prochazka, and Patricia Valdivia from the Education Ministry.

Acronyms and Abbreviations

APAFA	*Asociación de Padres de Familia*—Parents' Association
CEI	*Consejo Educativo Institucional*—School Governing Council
CENAPAFA	*Central Nacional de APAFAs*—National Parents' Association
CNE	*Consejo Nacional de Educación*—Nacional Education Council
COPALE	*Consejo Participativo Local de Educación*—Local Participatory Education Council (Provincial Level)
COPARE	*Consejo Participativo Regional de Educación*—Regional Participatory Education Council
DRE	*Dirección Regional de Educación*—Regional level school management and supervision unit
EIB	*Educación Intercultural Bilingüe*—Intercultural and Bilingual Education
ENAHO	*Encuesta Nacional de Hogares*—National Household Survey
ENDES	*Encuesta Demográfica y de Salud Familiar*—National Demographic and Family Health Survey (Peru's version of the DHS or Demographic Health Surveys)
FENAPAFA	*Federación Nacional de APAFAs*—National Federation of Parents' Associations
FyA	*Fe y Alegría*
FONCODES	*Fondo de Cooperación para el Desarrollo Social*—The National Social Investment Fund
FORMABIAP	*Formación de Maestros Bilingües de la Amazonía Peruana*—Bilingual Teacher Training for the Peruvian Amazon
LLECE	*Laboratorio Latinoamericano de Evaluación de la Calidad Educativa*—Latin American Laboratory for Evaluation of Education Quality
MINEDU	*Ministerio de Educación*—Ministry of Education of Peru
MRE	"Most recent estimate"
PEB	*Programa de Educación Bilingüe*—Bilingual Education Program
PEBIAN	*Programa de Educación Bilingüe Intercultural del Alto Napo*—Program for Bilingual Intercultural Education of the High Napo
PEEB	*Programa de Educación Experimental Bilingüe*—Project for Experimental Bilingual Education
PIRLS	Progress in International Reading Study
PISA	Programme for International Student Assessment
TIMSS	Trends in International Mathematics and Science Study
SIAF	*Sistema Integrado de Administración Financiera*—Integrated Financial Administration System
UGEL	*Unidad de Gestión Educativa Local*—Provincial level school management and supervision unit

Executive Summary

Current Situation

Peru has made great strides in educational coverage. Gross enrollment ratios at all schooling levels are higher than (or, within measurement error, as high as) those in countries with similar per capita income in Latin America. Completion rates are high—nearly 100 percent in primary school, and around 65 percent in secondary. Although the gender balance is not perfect, it is at about the same level as that found in the rest of Latin America. In truth, it has to be recognized that some of this enrollment takes place in schools where the quality of infrastructure is less than optimal, and so one might question the nature of this coverage. Nonetheless, overall, coverage is high. Furthermore, most students who do not finish high school are constrained from finishing by economic (poverty, fees, the need to work), social (pregnancy or marriage, youths alienation and gang behavior), and educational quality (school is not seen to be useful) problems, not by the unavailability of schools.

However, Peru has a quality problem, as proxied by levels of learning. It has participated in two international comparisons of learning achievement, PISA and LLECE. On PISA, Peru's scores were the lowest in Latin America (about 20 percent behind the average of Chile, Argentina, Brazil, and Mexico), and were far behind those of other middle-income countries with growing educational achievement, such as Thailand, with which Peru will have to compete. Only about 5 percent of Peru's students perform at the OECD average. Peru's own national student assessments yield disappointing results, with only some 20 percent of students performing at the desired level. In our own simple reading assessment, again, only about 20 percent of students in grades 1 and 2 were performing at a reasonable level. It is important to keep in mind that Peru also has fairly low income per capita, a relatively high demographic burden, and relatively low levels of literacy in the parental and grand-parental generations. Thus, the average level of student performance is not very surprising. More interesting is the fact that there is great inequality in performance in Peru, and that a significant gap exists between enrollment levels and performance. In mathematics, for example, and taking both PISA and TIMSS, Peru's internal inequality of results was the highest after South Africa. Furthermore, unlike in most countries, inequality in Peru cannot be explained solely in economic terms. Other factors, such as linguistic or cultural discrimination or a lack of attention to pedagogical development for the poor, seem to be at work. Furthermore, inequality in learning achievement *among* the poor is higher than inequality among the better-off. In fact, inequality among the poor themselves is half as high as inequality between the poor and the rich. There is neither micro nor macro evidence that low and highly variable quality among the poor is mostly due to resource constraints. All this strongly suggests that the problem is a lack of standards and accountability, which is accompanied by a dearth of models for effective pedagogy and other forms of support (for example, nutritional supplementation) for the poor. Finally, the contrast between achievement and enrollment in Peru is very high. In most countries with high enrollment ratios, achievement is also reasonably high. This is not so in Peru: there is a great imbalance between enrollment levels and what youths actually learn. This most likely means that the labor market will have trouble absorbing many youths who are being led to believe they are educated but who do not, in truth, know very much. The consequences for social cohesion and tranquility are impossible to predict but are unlikely to be good.

The determinants of quality and learning appear to be the following, in order of priority: quality of management and work effort, poverty, language of origin, and resource provision. The education sector can do much about the first and third factors. It can improve management, quality and work effort levels. It can also address issues of appropriate pedagogy for children whose first language is not Spanish. Poverty is harder to address with sectoral policies, evidently. It will require some cross-sectoral collaboration, as well as broad economic growth. It would also help if there were more pro-poor spending of a transparent nature, especially on the resources that are known to make a difference. But the most important addressable issue is the very poor quality of management in the sector.

The issue of pedagogical models for the approximately one quarter of children whose main home language is not Spanish is important but daunting. Results show that language of origin is, after management and poverty, an important and independent determinant of learning achievement. There have been some ten major efforts to improve bilingual education. Yet, very limited systemic evaluation has been conducted on these efforts, and as such relatively little is known about how to handle this issue.

Spending on education in Peru, which is around 3 percent of GDP, is low in comparison with other countries. Although spending has been relatively efficient in generating coverage, it has not been efficient in generating quality. Peru is near the limit of what countries can do to generate coverage via spending, but it is considerably below the limit, or even the average, of what countries can do to turn spending into learning achievement. Furthermore, spending patterns are inefficient: too much is spent on salaries, and not enough on other forms of support. Salaries have been increased across the board in Peru over the last few years, but there is no evident reciprocal commitment from teacher interest groups to improve quality or to be evaluated (though there appears to be some recent change in the right direction). Finally, there are no indicator or standards systems in use to allow managers to relate spending to quality or to allow individual users to know whether the system is delivering; in effect, there are few if any quality control systems and there is certainly no management of value-for-money. Under these circumstances, it seems unwise to attempt to simply spend one's way into quality. Yet, this seems to be the dominant tendency in Peru. The key social pact in the education sector—created in the last few years—has only one numerical goal: spending. It does have some quality goals, but these are not numerically specified and there is no general consensus on what they ought to be. Additionally, no causal mechanism is posited, in these policies and plans, between spending increases and the quality improvement that is hoped for. Finally, it is apparent that the relatively low spending on education in Peru is not a matter of sectoral prioritization within the public budget but instead an issue of low fiscal effort. Thus, while Peru may ultimately have to spend more on education in order to improve quality, this spending is likely to be very difficult to generate and also hard to manage properly under current conditions. Part of the low fiscal effort is likely due to the fact that economic authorities and the taxpayers distrust the public management of quality in service provision. Thus, a more fruitful way to proceed is likely to first require an improvement in quality control systems and quality management systems geared at generating confidence in the tax-paying public and in the economic authorities that the spending can be well-managed.

Policy Recommendations

Given the diagnosis outlined above, the following policy recommendations come to the fore.

Standards

First, Peru needs to establish much clearer and more specific learning standards.[1] Specificity needs to refer to both the grade level and clarity of goals. For example, goals should exist at a minimum by grade, and ideally by semester. Goals should be stated in specific terms, such as measuring levels of comprehension, fluency, and specific numerical skills. Standards should be simple enough so that parents and teachers can understand them. Plenty of examples need to be created and distributed so that the actors can see the standards embodied in materials. Reading materials of standardized grade or age appropriateness, suitable for take-home or pleasure reading, need to be created and distributed. Quality goals for secondary education could be embodied in a national secondary-school-leaving exam or certification. Peru also needs to establish service and process standards—meaning standards of behavior (such as hours of effective and active learning per year) and for reporting to the clients—in a process of downward accountability of schools to communities and of the Province-level School Management and Supervision Unit (*Unidad de Gestión Educativa Local,* UGELs) to schools. Provision standards need to be developed whereby, for example, funding formulas are developed for the national level to fund regions and for regions to fund schools. Funding according to formulas is more transparent, equitable and efficient than the current totally *ad hoc* funding (if the formulas are simple and transparent). For example, formulas could be based quite simply on enrollment and poverty. Finally, clear and rigorous standards for teachers are needed as part of a strategy for upgrading teacher quality significantly over time. Standards for both recruitment and professional behavior should be used, and can include the accreditation of teacher training approaches at colleges and universities. These standards should include subject-matter knowledge and could be incorporated in the *Carrera Pública Magisterial* or its regulations.

The need to create standards is related to the need to develop a culture of evaluation in Peru. There is currently a pervasive fear in Peru's education sector of anyone being

---

1. Since the word "standards" is used throughout this document, it is important to offer some definitions. First, in the context of learning, by "standards" we mean both a system of measurement or "metrics", such as a way of measuring a student's performance (e.g., words read correctly per minute), as well as a specific numerical goals to be achieved (e.g., being able to read 60 words per minute by the end of grade 2) or non-numerical skills to be learned (e.g., learning letter-sound recognition). Other such metrics and goals exist, of course. Second, in the context of management and funding processes, we refer to standardized ways of proceeding, such as funding via formulas, as well as specific goals such as saying that each school should receive so many soles per child for purchasing learning materials. Having standardized ways for schools to report on budget use to parents is another example of a process standard. Third, in the context of bilingual education, we refer to standardization of languages of instruction in order to discuss the limits to standardization. It would be possible to state, each time the word or concept is used, the exact meaning intended. However, given the pervasiveness of the use of the concept, it would also be tedious. The expectation is that the context will make it clear enough. In any case, what the appropriate notion of standard might be is open to discussion and interpretation. For example, while we believe we should recommend that children be able to correctly read 60 words per minute by the end of grade 2 (a standard as an actual goal), the policy dialogue process in Peru might determine that for now it is wisest simply to get teachers to track students on this measurement and try to improve it (a standard as a metric).

evaluated. This creates a vicious cycle. The fear of failure creates a fear of evaluation, but the lack of evaluation condemns almost all efforts to failure, because there is no serious way to detect when anything is going wrong. Failure and lack of evaluation against any kind of standard become mutual self-fulfilling prophecies and create an environment of intense pessimism, fatalism, and non-accountability. The fear of evaluation and standards has been turned into a virtue, and it has become popular to question evaluation and measurement as intellectually suspect, non-modern, regressive, or inequality-inducing. This pessimism, however, is most likely largely unjustified. It is shown in this study that there are many schools that perform well, and that high expectations are often met by high performance. Having clear and reasonably high expectations is an important way to break the vicious cycle of pessimism and the games of blame-the-child or blame-society that seem to be pervasive in Peru.

Accountability

Second, Peru needs to develop much clearer lines of accountability pressure and consumer or parental power. Without accountability pressure and rewards ("incentives"), agents will not come to standard (and without standards, accountability pressure is unable to determine what direction to seek). Given the situation of low accountability that has developed in Peru over the past decades, most teachers will not, for example, spend the hours of effort required to come to standard if they are not supervised and motivated by both communities and bureaucracy, and if expectations are not made clear. Some will make the effort needed and already do so, motivated by intrinsic professionalism and pride (as documented in this report); most, however, neither make the effort now nor will do so in the future unless accountability patterns are changed. Parents should have more say in what happens in schools, helping to decide on issues such as the use of school budgets and the selection of teachers and careers. Options such as giving parents a statutory majority on the School Governing Council (*Consejo Educativo Institucional,* CEIs) and giving the CEIs more power in determining teacher selection and teacher evaluation should be considered. Another alternative could be to give more power to the APAFAs to demand quality accountability in various ways, including teacher appraisal. The right of parents to have their children learn to a certain standard should be strongly disseminated and discussed. An important tool of accountability will be to strongly encourage the less motivated and capable teachers to leave the profession (or even find ways to dismiss them). This would increase the turnover rate and would allow new teachers into the system, and if the latter have met knowledge standards, the quality of the profession would improve faster. Finally, more systemic and evaluated experimentation in outsourcing of education for the poor, such as the *FyA* model, should be carried out, though it would be naive to expect any miracles from this experimentation for reasons documented later in this report.

Support

Third, support needs to be improved so that actors can come to standard. Accountability pressure and the specification of standards are not enough if agents lack appropriate information and the ability to come to standard in the first place. Pressure without outlets will only frustrate agents and clients. However, more teacher support and training of the traditional variety will not be useful. Teacher training, both in-service and pre-service, has tended to be too generic, too theoretical and (in the case of in-service training) too episodic, precisely because there are no sufficiently clear learning standards. Instead, much more specific in-service training is needed—training that accompanies the teacher throughout the year and which is focused on orienting the teacher in the year-long process to help students achieve annual learning goals. In short, the training needs to be child-centered, not teacher-centered. Similarly, much more and better learning materials, in particular reading materials, libraries, stationery, and supplies are required. Both of these types of support will be expensive. Thus, general financial support is also needed; education expenditure as a share of gross domestic product (GDP) will likely have to increase. However, this should not take place until standards and accountability systems are created and functioning. Most of the first tranches of any increased spending should be focused on the development and capacity building needed to implement these systems. Support itself needs to be standardized. For example, intergovernmental funding systems and school grants should be set in terms of simple formulas that are transparent and clear in their intent, perhaps with only two drivers: enrollment and poverty.

CHAPTER 1

Overview of Current Indicators

This chapter lays out the main indicators characterizing Peru's education system. Coverage, learning results, and equity are the focus.

Coverage

Looked at from any angle, Peru has achieved an impressive degree of education coverage. Table 1.1 shows the basic coverage data for the last few years in Peru and, where relevant or available, the most recent estimate for Latin America.

As can be seen, coverage in Peru is high compared to the rest of Latin America. Similar to other areas of Latin America with heavy indigenous presence, Peru is a little behind on gender equity. Even so, the gender equity index is 98 percent (and, at 94 percent for secondary schooling, the situation is not much worse than in primary).

One can make more fine-tuned benchmarks than simply comparing to the median for Latin America. Most education coverage statistics are quite correlated—in international comparisons—with income per capita, because educational development is part and parcel (from both demand and supply sides) of overall social and economic development. For example, the correlation between the secondary net enrollment ratio and GDP per capita is 0.65 for Latin American countries.[2] It is reasonable, therefore, to use GDP per capita as a way of fixing a reasonable level of expectation with regard to education indicators. In almost all cases, Peru's coverage indicators are above the value one would expect based on

---

2. Secondary net enrollment ratio measured in 2000, GDP per capita in US$ in exchange rate terms taken at the geometric average of the 1990s. Secondary net enrollment ratio sourced from EDSTATS, GDP per capita from SIMA.

Table 1.1. Education System Coverage Data for Peru and Latin America as a Whole

	1998	1999	2000	2001	2002	2003	2004	Latin America Most Recent Available Data
				Peru				
Gross Enrollment Ratios, public and private, not including adult education programs								
Pre-primary	57%	57%	59%	60%	61%	60%	63%	58%
Primary	120%	121%	119%	118%	117%	116%	114%	110%
Secondary	82%	83%	86%	89%	90%	89%	90%	79%
Tertiary	29%	30%	30%	31%	32%	33%	33%	24%
Net Enrollment Ratios, public and private								
Pre-primary	NA	NA	NA	NA	NA	NA	NA	NA
Primary	100%	100%	100%	100%	100%	NA	NA	93%
Secondary	61%	62%	63%	67%	67%	NA	NA	69%
Tertiary	NA	NA	NA	NA	NA	NA	NA	NA
Completion proxies (enrollment in terminal year minus repetition that year)								
Primary	97%	101%	98%	97%	95%	98%	NA	93%
Secondary	58%	59%	56%	61%	63%	66%	NA	NA
Shares of private enrollment in total enrollment								
Primary	13%	12%	13%	13%	14%	14%	14%	15%
Secondary	16%	16%	16%	16%	16%	17%	16%	24%
Tertiary	42%	41%	40%	41%	41%	43%	NA	NA
Gender parity index (ratio of female gross enrollment ratio to male gross enrollment ratio)								
Primary and secondary together	97%	97%	97%	97%	97%	97%	98%	101%

Sources: For Peru, derived from *Ministerio de Educación, Unidad de Estadística Educativa, Cifras de la Educación 1998–2004.* For Latin America, EDSTATS. Data for Latin America are the medians, across all countries, of the most recent available data *for each single country,* thus the group averages are not used.

some measure of GDP per capita. Again, to use the net secondary enrollment rate as an example, the expected value for Peru would have been 54 percent in 2000, but as shown in the table above, the actual value was already 63 percent in 2000.[3] Peru has had secondary enrollment ratios (both net and gross) similar to, or higher than, those of countries with considerably higher per capita income, such as Mexico, Colombia, or Costa Rica.[4] Similarly,

---

3. The expected value has to be calculated for 2000 because this is the last year for which a large amount of data for the rest of Latin America is available, and the expectation is based on looking at data for all of Latin America.

4. Costa Rican data available at http://www.mep.go.cr/CuadroEscolaridadHistorico.html on November 6, 2004. Mexican data available through the interactive software *Sistema para el Análisis de la Estadística Educativa, Secretaría de Educación Pública.* Colombian data available at http://www.mineducacion.gov.co/index2.html on November 6, 2004.

Peru's expected primary completion rate in 2000 would have been 88 percent, but Peru had already achieved 98 percent completion by 2000. Finally, at around 66 percent (the 2003 values are an estimate) secondary completion is very high, which is to be expected given how high gross tertiary enrollment is.

Not only are the coverage values high, but many of the coverage indicators have grown somewhat faster than for the rest of Latin America in the period 1990 to 2001 (the last year for which there are comprehensive data for the whole continent). As Table 1.1 shows, most indicators have risen over the last few years. Progress has been maintained, except in areas where further upward movement is not reasonable, such as in the gross enrollment ratio for primary schooling.

Learning and Quality

Given the difficulty of defining education quality, a frequently used proxy is learning achievement on some standardized test. Peru has participated in two such tests: PISA 2000 and LLECE. The PISA 2000 test is perhaps more useful as a benchmark because it includes a wider variety of countries. Peru's performance on PISA 2000 (taking overall reading ability, mathematics ability, and science ability together, as a simple average) was worse than that of any other participating country, including the other developing countries in the sample. Peru's average score on the three PISA 2000 components (reading, mathematics, and science) was 16 percent below Brazil and 23 percent below Mexico. These results were met with consternation in Peru. However, it is important to put things in perspective. Peru was one of the poorest countries participating in PISA 2000 and was also one of the countries in the sample making the most recent transition to mass literacy.

Of all countries included in PISA 2000, Peru had the second highest youth dependency ratio (population 0–14 over population 15–64). If one takes these disadvantage factors into account simultaneously, Peru's performance on PISA 2000 was only somewhat worse than expected, as shown in Figure 1.1 below. There is, furthermore, a scaling problem in most graphical depictions of Peru's position on PISA 2000 (including in the original PISA 2000 reports from the OECD). Given that Peru was the worst performer, if the origin of the axis is drawn at some arbitrary

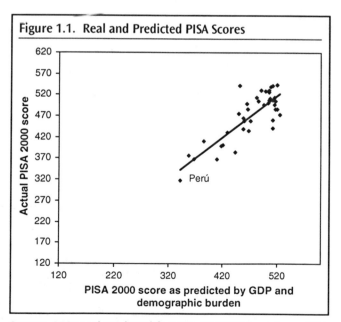

Figure 1.1. Real and Predicted PISA Scores

Source: OECD and UIS (2003) for PISA, EDSTATS for data on GDP and demography. Analysis performed by the author.

point below Peru's performance, then the gap between Peru's performance and its expected performance, even controlling for various factors, appears very large. But this is partly because the origin is arbitrary in most such depictions. In the figures below we have used what we believe is a more reasonable origin.[5] Thus, put into perspective, Peru's average performance is not as low as often thought. The real problems are elsewhere.

Given how far Peru has come in terms of access to secondary school, and that it is somewhat below expectations on quality, an outcome issue of real interest is the gap between coverage and quality, or between access and learning. Figure 1.2 illustrates this point quite clearly.[6] It is to be noted that "Asian Tigers" are typically on the dividing line, or even further on the other side of the dividing line or central tendency between access and learning performance as Peru: they typically have paid relatively more attention to how much children are learning than to raw access, though their access numbers are also very good. The positions of Thailand and Korea are illustrated to contrast with that of Peru. Peru is an outlier on the "bad" side of the divide.

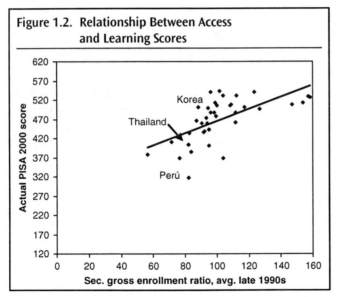

Figure 1.2. Relationship Between Access and Learning Scores

Sources: OECD and UIS (2003) for PISA 2000 data, EDSTATS for enrollment ratio data.

Thus, one peculiar feature of education outcomes in Peru is the large gap between access and learning. While it would be speculative to state that this will lead to social unrest due to unmet (and unjustifiable) expectations created by high-school completion—which currently means little—it is certainly an issue to be concerned about.

A related gap is that between the performance of Peru's worst-performers and those of other countries. The two graphs below show the cumulative and relative frequency of performance in the PISA 2000 reading test (the "combined reading scale") in Peru, other developing countries, and the OECD. Two facts are worthy of note. First, from Figure 1.4, which shows the cumulative frequencies of proficiency, we can note that only the very best-performing (about 5 percent) Peruvian

---

5. The common practice in many such graphs is to use some arbitrary round number below the lowest score, in this case Peru. We have instead taken the distribution of Peru's own scores at the key centiles, and projected performance at the lowest possible centile in the distribution, using a polynomial fit. This projects a hypothetical "worst case" that is a reasonably proxy for an "absolute zero." The mean of various polynomial estimates was 120, and this is taken as the most meaningful zero level for graphical display.

6. The axes have been re-scaled to make the relative scale of the two graphs identical, so that the distance of Peru to the central tendency in both cases can be more easily compared.

children perform in the range of the OECD average. But the most important issue is the underperformance of Peru's worst performers. More than half of Peruvian children are not even at the first level of proficiency in reading ability. It is clear that countries that are developing well educationally, and that have made well-recognized efforts to improve educational quality, seem to have compressed the percentage of children at this level. This is visible in the shape of both the cumulative and simple (Figure 1.3 frequency distributions. Thailand stands out as a good performer and, in Latin America, Mexico does as well.

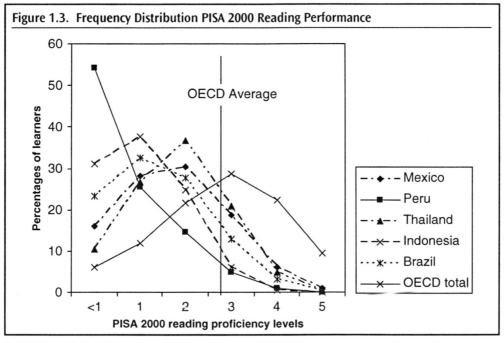

Figure 1.3. Frequency Distribution PISA 2000 Reading Performance

Source: Graphed from OECD and UIS (2003).

Finally, of all countries in PISA 2000, Peru had the highest ratio of variance to average performance, taking mathematical literacy as the key index this time. Either this ratio, or the ratio of performance at the 95th to performance at the 5th percentiles, can be taken as indices of educational inequality. We use the latter. As noted, Peru had the worst ratio for educational inequality in the PISA 2000 sample. If one adds data for other countries from other international mathematical tests, namely the TIMSS 1999 and 2003 (for a total of some 14 developing countries, depending on how one counts), Peru's performance on PISA 2000 shows more inequality than any other country's performance on any of these three international tests, with the exception of South Africa's performance on either TIMSS. Moreover, this index of educational inequality is, in most countries, fairly well correlated with the Gini coefficient of income inequality. Peru, however, is an outlier, as Figure 1.5 shows: the level of educational inequality in Peru (at least by this measure) is considerably above what its level of income inequality in the 1990s would have predicted. It is possible that Peru is not an outlier. Perhaps Peru, along with a few other countries, is on a different line determined by third factors not captured in this graphic. The other near-outlier country

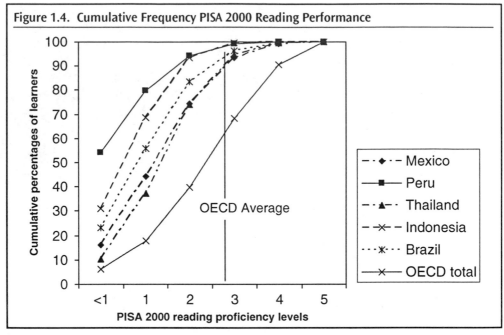

Figure 1.4. Cumulative Frequency PISA 2000 Reading Performance

Source: Graphed OECD and UIS (2003).

on the chart is Israel (half as far above the line as Peru and at a Gini coefficient of about 35). Another country that would be an outlier (but whose data is from TIMSS rather than PISA so it is not graphed) is South Africa, with an educational inequality index, on this variable, of approximately 4.2, but a Gini coefficient of around 60. These facts (Peru, Israel to some degree, and South Africa being outliers) suggest that there may indeed be some countries for which a special relationship is needed: there is, perhaps, a third dimension in Figure 1.5 and Peru may lie on a well-fitted line in that dimension. This emphasizes the point that there is something social or curricular about Peru's educational inequality that goes beyond the sorts of generic economic inequalities normally associated with Gini coefficients. (An alternative but equivalent interpretation is that sociological and cultural inequalities in Peru are not well correlated with economic inequalities.) The thought that one may be in the company of South Africa should be a sobering realization, given this country's past and present ethnic divisions and tensions.

In summary, Peru has done well in expanding education coverage. Coverage levels are high compared to the rest of Latin America, and compared to what one would expect based on GDP per capita. Not all children finish secondary school; only about 65 percent do. This number might be considered relatively high by Latin American standards, and is high relative to the low quality of the education Peruvian students receive. Nonetheless, the issue of why students do not finish is of interest and is covered in Chapter 5. Peruvian children learn somewhat less than one would predict given the country's level of per capita GDP and its demographic burden. There is also a very large gap between coverage and learning. Peru has a definite problem in that it is producing large numbers of high-school graduates with very poor cognitive skills. When countries produce as many secondary school graduates as Peru does, the cognitive skills of these graduates should be much higher than they

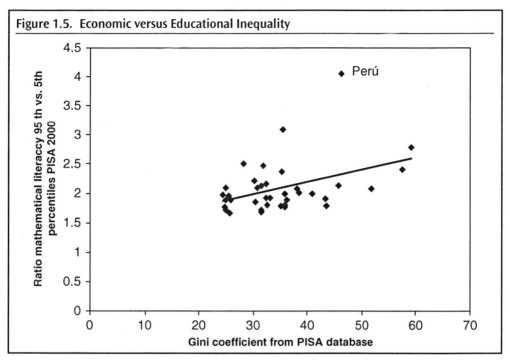

Figure 1.5. Economic versus Educational Inequality

Source: Graphed from data in OECD and UIS (2003).

currently are in Peru. The gap between numbers and skills may create a crisis of expectations. In a related manner, there is a large gap between the percentage of children at very low levels of proficiency in Peru and the percentages seen at the same level in other countries (or, alternatively, the gap between those who learn the most in Peru and those who learn the least is very large if one considers how low the average levels of learning are). Furthermore, this high level of educational inequality is not explainable in terms of Peru's overall economic inequality. These are the outcome problems Peru has to contend with. The possible determinants of these problems are discussed in the following chapters.

CHAPTER 2

Educational Diagnostics and Recommendations

The previous chapter has argued that the remaining problems in Peru's education sector are largely related to learning achievement, and in particular to the low and extremely variable levels of learning achievement among the poor.

This chapter will argue that there is no shortage of lists of clear recommendations about how to improve the education system in Peru. There is also no dearth of research studies upon which to base policy recommendations. The strong implication is that basic knowledge about "what to do" is not, in general terms, much of a constraint to improvement. The chapter will then suggest that there are two real constraints. First, a lack of willingness to do what the research suggests should be done and second, a certain absence of knowledge on *how* to do what needs to be done.

Stock of Peruvian Research on "What Works" in Schooling

A good stock of policy prescriptions already exists in Peru, as will be seen below. This stock of policy recommendations is not based on mere opinion. In the last decade the Peruvian literature on the factors associated with improved learning has grown quickly. The capacity of the education system, or of intellectuals vaguely associated with the education system, to diagnose itself is far greater than the system's actual capacity to use these diagnoses (through policy and administrative change), perhaps to a degree unusual in Latin America (see Table 2.1).

This literature is of high quality, and its conclusions are fairly firm—it is possible to discern a common thread of explicit or implicit policy suggestions coming out of the research. This section discusses the main findings. It does not pretend to cover the entire Peruvian literature on this subject, as many of the findings echo each other.[7]

The basic factors identified in this literature fall into four broad groups:

1. Poverty as such, but also a lack of attention to the needs of particular sub-populations, in particular the poor, and specifically the poor of non-Spanish-speaking origin. This lack of attention seems to have two dimensions. First, lack of appropriate cultural and pedagogical models that are proven to boost learning among the poor and those whose mother tongue is not Spanish. Second, the fact that the problems of poor quality of teaching, and lack of standards and accountability, are worst among the poor.

2. Poor quality of teachers, poor quality of teaching. These quality problems appear to be fundamental, and appear to be related to basic lack of skills among teachers. These issues appear difficult to correct with traditional "teacher-training" methods, and most likely have to do with teacher selection and motivation. As will be seen in later sections, added to this is an over-ambitious and conceptually complex curriculum that is probably too difficult for teachers in rural areas to apply, at least with the currently meager levels of problem-specific support (as opposed to superficial, generic in-service training).

3. Poor time-on-task, low coverage of the curriculum, low effort, all due to a lack of standards and standard enforcement, or a lack of accountability.

4. Lack of parental involvement, low accountability to parents, low ability of parents to pressure schools on quality issues, partly due to a lack of standards.

Somewhat absent are strong research results that suggest scarcity of resources (aside from scarcity of skilled teachers working devotedly) is a major problem. Some studies, along with our own analysis (shown below), do suggest a minor role for resources. As is shown in other chapters of this report, if one looks at the school level, it is not clear that the poor are under-resourced, relatively speaking, in terms of the most expensive factors, such as the pupil-teacher ratio; it is clear, however, that they under-resourced in terms of *capable* teachers. It is also shown that learning results are much more poorly distributed than, say, raw teacher resources (the pupil-teacher ratio). The apparent lack of relationship between raw resources and learning results may have two causes. First, in some cases there may indeed be no relationship. This is likely the case with teacher costs, because teacher costs, in the current compensation scheme in Peru, do not reward teacher quality. Second, studies of the type shown below rely on variation in order to estimate effects. If all schools get more or less the same

---

7. In general, results in Table 2.2 and Table 2.3 are reported only if they are statistically significant at the 5 percent level or better, and if they tend to show up in more than one subject matter and in more than just one or two model specifications. Factors tending to appear only in one study, or in one subject, or in one model specification, are not reported. In cases where there are several variables that have a significance level worse than 5 percent, but better than 10 percent, and are most likely highly correlated with each other, we suspect multi-collinearity and report the factor in any case (e.g., if father's education, socioeconomic status, expectations that the student will complete secondary school, and expectations that the student will attend university all appear with low significance, we assume all of these largely refer to socioeconomic status and report the latter). None of these analyses carry out a cost-effectiveness analysis of the identified factors.

amount of supplies (for example, if all schools get the basic textbooks, or if none do) then it is difficult to identify an impact from the presence or lack of textbooks. This does not mean that textbooks are unimportant, it simply means that their importance is hard to ascertain from quantitative studies of this sort. In short, while much research exists, it is important to take the results cautiously, particularly on the resource issue.

The resource issue raises one additional problem or puzzle. Poverty and socioeconomic status (SES) matters a great deal in determining learning results. In some studies, and in our own re-analysis of the data (shown below), poverty and general SES matter more than anything else in explaining learning results. Why, then, do public resources, which could be considered a way of making up for poverty or lack of private resources, seem not to matter as much? Aside from the possibilities already mentioned immediately above, the answer to this is unfortunately not clear, but we hypothesize it has to do with the fact that even private spending among the poor is not very efficient because consumers are underinformed or misinformed by their schools, whereas private spending among the better off is more efficient because this group finds ways to get reasonably standardized services and manages to establish comparative information about schools even if the government does not provide it (perhaps the fact that the less poor are more urban helps establish informal performance information and more competition between schools, as urban schools are much less able to establish a monopoly over their students). This issue is explored in subsequent chapters.

In order to summarize as many of these variables as is possible in one single source, and to give a direct flavor of what the research tends to show, we analyzed what is probably the most complete data set on schooling results and their determinants, the 2001 national evaluation results for 4th grades primary and secondary for Spanish ("comunicación integral") and Mathematics ("lógico-matemática"). This was done using Hierarchical Linear Modeling (HLM). A summary of the results is presented in Table 2.2 and in Table 2.3.[8] For variables whose p-value is less than 0.01 and whose standardized coefficient is greater than 0.05, we also classified the variables into just four broad groupings to make the results more intelligible. These classifications are shown. Finally, we then counted the number of times the broad groupings show up as correlates of learning in the four sets of results (mathematics and Spanish, in 4th grade primary and in 4th grade secondary). This final count provides a good snapshot of the broad issues that appear to be shaping learning results, at least according to this one instrument. Furthermore, these results are fully consistent with the review of existing literature already discussed above. The broad factors are:

1. Poverty and socioeconomic issues: 13 cases
2. School and classroom management, pedagogy, having norms and standards: 10 cases
3. Ethnic and gender disadvantage (above and beyond poverty): 5 cases
4. Resources and resource use: 3 cases

---

8. Variables that apply at the pupil level are symbolized with a (P), since we have not followed the traditional practice of segregating the school vs. student-level variables in the presentation. In this table, the results were first sorted by level of significance. Then, in order to be as rigorous as possible, variables whose p-value is less than 0.01 were sorted by the size of the standardized coefficient, that is, the "substantive" level of significance. Thus, variables with standardized coefficients greater than 0.05 and p-value less than 0.01 are sorted by the size of the standardized coefficient, whereas variables with p-value not less than 0.01 are simply sorted by the p-value.

Table 2.1. Factors Associated with Improved Learning Results in Peru

Factor	Discussion	Sources of evidence and range of application of the research	Possible policy implications
Coverage of the curriculum.	Coverage is very low but low coverage does not appear very related to poor achievement in a few studies, perhaps because higher coverage with poor quality does not add to achievement.	Cueto, Ramírez, León, and Pain (2003); 6th grade mathematics, Lima. Multivariate analysis. *Equipo de Análisis de la Unidad de Medición de la Calidad Educativa (2004)*. Multivariate analysis. Galindo (2002). Multivariate analysis.	Poor teacher preparation for certain areas, poor accountability and supervision.
Use of materials provided by Ministry, lack of materials other than textbooks.	Materials are distributed but underused. Coverage (percent of materials used) is associated with achievement. In addition materials arrive late. Learning materials are reported to be not very usable or used. Other supplies and stationery are not supplied.	Cueto, Ramírez, León, and Pain (2003); 6th grade mathematics, Lima. Multivariate analysis. Data from the present report suggest that students do not recognize text from the reading materials and the materials are late. Based on non-random but "representative" quantitative sample and field visits. Hunt (2001). Expert opinion based on non-random sample, non-quantitative samples.	Review and assess use and appropriateness of materials, reform and redesign materials.
Gender.	Being male is associated with higher achievement, all other things being controlled for, particularly in mathematics.	Cueto, Ramírez, and León (2003). Language and mathematics, Lima and Ayacucho, 3rd and 4th grades. Multivariate analysis. Cueto, Ramírez, León, and Pain (2003); 6th grade mathematics, Lima. Multivariate analysis. Benavides (2002). Multivariate, large sample.	Pedagogical practices might discriminate against girls. Cultural expectations may also play a role.
Date school opens	Positively associated with achievement. Most likely a proxy for overall good management and time on task.	*Equipo de Análisis de la Unidad de Medición de la Calidad Educativa (2004)*. Multivariate analysis. Cueto and Secada (2001). Multivariate analysis.	Policies on time-on-task (campaign for 1000 hours of effective instruction) exist but are weakly enforced.

Time on task, and time on task devoted to high-value activities. Amount of homework.	Time on task generally very low, un-enforced, unsupervised. It impacts learning. Amount of homework positively associated with results.	Cueto and Secada (2001). Multivariate analysis. Hunt (2001). Expert opinion based on non-random sample, non-quantitative samples. Data from this report suggest that teachers use time very unproductively. Quantitative, "representative" but non-random sample. Montero, Ames, Cabrera, Chirinos, Fernández Dávila, León. 2002. Small sample quantitative. Benavides (2002). Multivariate, large sample.	Policies on time-on-task (campaign for 1000 hours of effective instruction) exist but are weakly enforced.
Level of teaching and problem-setting in mathematics, poor or no feedback on problem sets. Teacher lack of confidence and incapacity in specific skills inreading and evaluation. Teachers are badly prepared in general.	Teachers correct problems lightly, and often give incorrect feedback to students. Quality of feedback and problems is associated with more achievement. Teachers do use standards, but they are informal and lower than they should be. On the other hand, instructional strategies and texts may be more complicated than necessary.	Cueto, Ramírez, León, and Pain (2003); 6th grade mathematics, Lima. Multivariate analysis. Hunt (2001). Expert opinion based on non-random sample, non-quantitative samples. Data from the present report suggest that teachers do use standards, but even if they were meeting goals fully, reading would still be below where it should be. Arregui (1996).	Teacher's own education is poor, due partly to selection of personnel into the profession. Support to teachers is insufficiently specific.
Spanish ability (and Spanish mother tongue)—affecting mathematics achievement as well.	Generally highly correlated with achievement. *In some models this is the only really significant factor.* Tends to appear significant even when general socioeconomic status and other educational factors are controlled for. EIB programs are generally poor, and education in areas where Spanish is not an ancestral language is generally poor. The indigenous/non-indigenous gap is worse in Peru than in Bolivia or Mexico.	Cueto (2003). Rural. Transition 4th to 6th grade. Controls for initial achievement. Multivariate analysis. *Equipo de Análisis de la Unidad de Medición de la Calidad Educativa (2004).* Multivariate analysis. Cueto and Secada (2001). Multivariate, rural. Sakellariou (2004), multivariate analysis based on LLECE results.	Lack of strong enough programs and methods for non-Spanish-speaking children. Need for value-added analysis and reasonable expectations.

(continued)

Table 2.1. Factors Associated with Improved Learning Results in Peru (*Continued*)

Factor	Discussion	Sources of evidence and range of application of the research	Possible policy implications
Socioeconomic status of family.	Often quite correlated with achievement. Probably co-linear with Spanish ability or language spoken at home, but often has significance independent of the latter. In some studies this is the most important measurable factor in driving student learning.	Cueto, Ramírez, and León (2003). Language and mathematics, Lima and Ayacucho, 3rd and 4th grades. Multivariate analysis. Benavides (2002). Multivariate, large sample. Data analysis for this report in Table 2.2 and Table 2.3.	Lack of compensatory mechanisms and resource targeting. Need for value-added analysis and reasonable expectations.
Cultural capital in the home (e.g., number of books).	Associated with increased achievement.	Benavides (2002). Multivariate, large sample.	Lack of compensatory programs and resource targeting. Need for value-added analysis and reasonable expectations.
Child labor.	Negatively associated with achievement even when socioeconomic status is controlled for.	*Equipo de Análisis de la Unidad de Medición de la Calidad Educativa (2004)*. Multivariate analysis.	Lack of compensatory mechanisms and resource targeting. Need for value-added analysis and reasonable expectations.
Level/quality of teacher training.	Somewhat associated with achievement. Could be a proxy for overall general knowledge and status of teachers.	Cueto (2003). Rural. Transition 4th to 6th grade. Controls for initial achievement. Multivariate analysis.	Teacher recruitment and retention.
Resources such as school libraries, reading materials at home, etc.	Some impact from these factors is found, as would be expected. Many of these factors probably have an effect, but the statistical significance is masked by the presence of other factors that are correlated, such as socioeconomic status of the family.	Benavides (2002). Multivariate, large sample. Evidence in analysis carried out for this report as presented in Table 2.2 and in Table 2.3.	Unclear. Conclusion should not be that material inputs do not matter, but that total resources, as opposed to specific resources, are a factor of secondary importance compared to the management of those resources.
Parental involvement in homework.	Could be a proxy for parental involvement in general.	*Equipo de Análisis de la Unidad de Medición de la Calidad Educativa (2004)*. Multivariate analysis.	Parental involvement in the past has generally been postulated as involving only assistance with infrastructure. Need for value-added analysis and reasonable expectations.

Table 2.2. Results on Determinants of Learning Based on 2001 National Evaluation

Spanish (*Comunicación Integral*) 4th Grade Primary

Broad Grouping	Variable	Std Coeff, Sig
SES	Socioecon index school	0.259***
SES	Rural	−0.138***
SES	Socioecon index pupils (P)	0.116***
Resources	School infrastructure index	0.116**
Ethnic/Gender	School in bilingual area	−0.102***
Management	Public School	−0.089**
Management	Curriculum Coverage	0.086***
SES	Whether pupil works Mon-Fri (P)	−0.084***
Management	Time spent by teacher preparing classes as % of total time worked	0.064***
Resources	School materials index	0.057**
SES	Mother's education (P)	0.052**
	Total teaching experience	0.04=
	Number of training courses taken by teacher per year	0.006*
	Percent repeaters	−0.052*
	Father's education (P)	0.036*
	Frequency of use of books in classroom by the teacher	0.034
	Teaching experience at school	−0.033
	Student's first language is Spanish (P)	0.036
	Parental satisfaction	0.052
	Expectation student will finish secondary school (P)	0.023
Percent variation explained		59%

Mathematics (*Lógico-Matemática*) 4th Grade Primary

Broad Grouping	Variable	Std Coeff, Sig
SES	Socioecon index school	0.387***
Management	Parental satisfaction	0.106**
SES	Socioecon index pupils (P)	0.088**
Ethnic/Gender	School in bilingual area	−0.078**
SES	Whether pupil works Mon-Fri (P)	−0.073***
Ethnic or Gender	Gender (P)	0.072***
Management	School starts year on time	0.064**
Ethnic/Gender	Student's first language is Spanish (P)	0.054**
Management	Time spent by teacher preparing classes as % of total time worked	0.053**
	Teacher experience at school	0.048***
	Father's education (P)	0.047**
	Expectation student will continue to tertiary (P)	0.037*
	Percent curriculum covered	0.049*
	Percent repeaters	−0.076*
	Month school received books	−0.055*
	Complimentary curriculum	0.052*
	Public School	−0.057*
	School infrastructure index	0.082*
	Expectation student will finish secondary (P)	0.028*
	Number of books in the household (P)	0.03
	Number of math tests	0.044
	Number of siblings (P)	−0.021
Percent variation explained		67%

Table 2.3. Results on Determinants of Learning Based on 2001 National Evaluation

Spanish (*Comunicación Integral*) 4th Grade Secondary			Mathematics (*Lógico-Matemática*) 4th Grade Secondary		
Broad Grouping	Variable	Std Coeff, Sig	Variable	Broad Grouping	Std Coeff, Sig
SES	Socioecon index school	0.499***	Socioecon index school	SES	0.356***
SES	Expectation student will continue to tertiary (P)	0.219***	Whether student likes Mathematics (P)	Student	0.141***
Resources	School materials index	0.065**	Gender (P)	Ethnic/gender	0.1***
Management	Public School	−0.063**	Public School	Management	−0.089**
	Pupil works weekends (P)	−0.042***	Coast	SES	−0.083***
	Number of books in the household (P)	0.039***	Expectation student will continue to tertiary (P)	SES	0.075***
	Curriculum Coverage	0.037**	Percentage of developed curricula competencies	Management	0.069***
	Student's first language is Spanish (P)	0.026**	Management of curricula contents (in percentages)	Management	0.053**
	Time pupil spends getting to school (P)	0.026***	Number of books in the household (P)		0.048***
	Gender (P)	0.026**	Age (P)		−0.022**
	Age (P)	−0.025**	Teacher experience		0.047*
	Student works Monday-Friday (P)	−0.02**	Father's education (P)		0.022*
	Father's education (P)	0.021*	Parental satisfaction		0.049*
	School starts year on time	0.035*	Student's first language is Spanish (P)		0.017*
	Complimentary curriculum	0.03*	No. of training courses taken by teacher since 1998		0.034
	Coast	−0.032*	Parents help with homework (P)		0.037
	Parental satisfaction	0.03	School infrastructure index		−0.042
	Rural	−0.025	Student works weekends (P)		−0.013
			Mother's education (P)		−0.014
Percent variation explained		49%	Percent variation explained		45%

It should be noted that poverty is far and away the most important determinant in almost all cases. In almost every case, it has the highest statistical or substantive significance.

The data source used, unlike those used in other studies such as Cueto and Secada (2001), Cueto, Ramírez, León, and Pain (2003), or Hunt (2001), does not allow a fine-grained look at issues related to the quality of instruction. Even so, issues of standards and school and classroom management appear high on this list. It is likely that if these factors had been taken into account in this survey, then issues related to school and classroom management and pedagogy would appear higher on this list.

It is likely that all these factors interact. For example, the lack of norms and standards (such as poor time on task) is probably worse among the poor. Similarly, the lack of proven pedagogical models is worse for those whose mother language is not Spanish. Thus, the disadvantages are cumulative, and it is easy to understand why children who are poor, whose mother language is not Spanish, and whose teachers are not very devoted and do not know how to use an effective pedagogy, are not learning much. Later chapters will document these issues in much more detail.

Existing Stock of Policy Suggestions

The Peruvian education system responds to policy suggestions, albeit incompletely, with a considerable lag, and more in certain areas than in others. For example, in the past few years there has been considerable progress in certain areas. Quality measurement, as proxied by learning achievement, albeit on a sample basis, has been implanted. (Though its funding tends to be dependent on outside influences.) General management information systems, such as enrollment counts and basic indicators, have greatly improved. Similarly, there have been improvements in payroll management, clean-up of ghost teachers, and some rationalization of teacher supply so that it matches enrollment-based needs. These are responses to obvious need and to policy recommendations made in the early through late 1990s.

There are many current lists of policy suggestions, including quite a few that have not yet been taken up. These vary from those produced by Peruvian and individual foreign expert analysis and opinion, to those based on international organizations' analyses, to those derived from consensus-building and large-scale consultation exercises within Peru. Most of these converge on a fairly consistent set of recommendations. Just in the 1990s and 2000s, one can cite World Bank (2001), Alcázar (2004), Hunt (2001), PREAL (2003), Francke (2004), Rodríguez (2004), Rivero (2004), Vega (2004), and, *Foro del Acuerdo Nacional (2004)* as examples of sets of policy suggestions. Table 2.4 is laid out so as to emphasize the range of agreement of all the various diagnostics and sets of recommendations. In the table, the fact that a symbol does not appear under an author's name does not imply the author does not support the idea; it simply implies that he or she does not discuss it—some of the papers do not present comprehensive lists of what the author thinks ought to be done to improve the system. In some cases (see for example, Cruz, Espinosa, Montané, and Rodríguez 2002), the authors do not lay out recommendations as such on the topic in question, but their description of a problem is so pointed and specific that it can be taken as an implicit recommendation. Finally, in a few cases, the interpretation of the authors' recommendations is not clear. This is symbolized with a question mark.

Table 2.4. Summary of Policy Recommendations in Some Key Peruvian Literature and Literature on Peru

Issue	Alcázar (2004)	Hunt (2001)	PREAL (2003)	Foro Acuerdo Nacional (2004)	Francke (2004)	Cruz, Espinosa, Montané, and Rodríguez (2002)	Vega (2004)	World Bank (2001)	Rivero (2004)
Establish more detailed and clearer performance expectations and standards.	✓	✓	✓			✓	✓	✓	
Increase capacity to demand and use standardized achievement testing, perhaps universalize testing in somegrades, some recommend dissemination of school-wise information.	✓	✓	✓	✓ (?)			✓	✓	
Make schools and teachers more accountable to parents and/or principals, including input into teacher evaluation by parents and principals.	✓	✓	✓		✓		✓		
Increase spending on education.	✓	✓	✓						✓
Target spending toward the poor, create more targeted programs, not just targeted spending.	✓	✓	✓					✓	✓
Clarify and finalize powers and functions under decentralization, including school autonomy, with fully specified responsibilities.	✓	✓	✓		✓				

Improve teacher pay (in some cases stated thus, in other cases stated only in relation to performance or specific skills).	✓ (?)	✓		✓
Simplify teacher reward system, make it more based on some measure of performance, including school-level evaluations.	✓	✓		✓
Rationalize and accredit pre-service teacher training, make it more selective.	✓	✓		✓
Increase coverage of pre-primary schooling.	✓	✓		✓
Evaluate existing and past pilot projects and initiatives, and force accountability to absorb lesson that work and reject those that do not.		✓	✓	
Simplify and clarify organization of the sector. Re-orient it so it serves the pedagogical functions.	✓	✓		✓
Ensure communitarian or administrative systems to guarantee attendance of teachers and students.		✓	✓	
Take steps to ensure continuity of policies and perhaps of Ministers.		✓		
Social mobilization around learning, specifically reading		✓		

(continued)

Table 2.4. Summary of Policy Recommendations in Some Key Peruvian Literature and Literature on Peru (*Continued*)

Issue	Alcázar (2004)	Hunt (2001)	PREAL (2003)	*Foro Acuerdo Nacional* (2004)	Francke (2004)	Cruz, Espinosa, Montané, and Rodríguez (2002)	Vega (2004)	World Bank (2001)	Rivero (2004)
Focus in particular on early literacy through expectations and programs.		✓							
Establish better methods and tools, including more reliable and standardized approaches, for education in non-Spanish-speaking areas.							✓	✓	
Clarify formulas for resource allocation to sub-national entities.					✓				
Ensure competitive selection and evaluation of sector managers.					✓				
Develop more specific, problem-oriented teacher support, instead of generic in-service training.	✓								

The most important conclusion to be derived from the analysis of the table below is that perhaps half of the recommendations have to do with accountability. This is not surprising given the research results discussed above. The rest have to do with support. However, both effective support and accountability require standards, and accountability requires the existence of measurement. Support also requires standards, given that it ought to be directed at helping actors perform to standard. Without standards it is difficult to say what the training and support should be about, and whether it has achieved anything. Thus, a close analysis of, and reflection on, the recommendations imply, as a foundation, a focus on: a) developing standards, b) improving mechanisms to hold service providers accountable for meeting standards, and c) improved support to help providers come to standard. A few recommendations, such as increased expenditure, or more emphasis on early childhood education, do not relate to either accountability or standards.

It is also important to note where there tends to be a lack of consensus. The more official documents tend to relatively underemphasize issues of standards, and tend to emphasize resource provision, narrower curricular and support matters, and more ambitious styles of pedagogy (for example, integration of areas of knowledge, critical thinking about learning itself, as themes in the curriculum). Almost all of the more official recommendations as to policy actions are purely qualitative or directional, and do not represent quantitative goals, *except*, pointedly, those that refer to more funding (for example, *Foro del Acuerdo Nacional 2004*, which sets a quantitative spending goal, but is silent on any quantitative results that could be delivered for this spending). Analysts coming from think tanks and academic environments, on the other hand, tend to emphasize some form of standards or accountability.

An important point to note with regard to Table 2.4 is that there is some disagreement between the best research and the policy recommendations. For example, the issue of *specific* support to teachers (how to teach to standards) to accompany improved or more specific standards tends to receive clear and strong attention from only one of the policy-recommendation authors as shown in the table, whereas the same issue receives quite a bit of attention from authors writing up research or empirical findings (Table 2.3 above).

Remaining Impediments

The evidence presented in the previous two sections suggests that at this point the main constraint to improved education results in Peru is not more research and more policy analysis—at least not along the lines already carried out. There is already a large stock of research-based suggestions. There is also a reserve of pilot projects and experiments. In the EIB area alone, for example, there are at least ten projects from which more could be learned, or could have been learned had these projects been more thoroughly evaluated (see Chapter 8).

There are some remaining knowledge problems, and a major policy problem.

First, it is true that there are some lacunae in knowledge. There seem to be three main types of knowledge lacking. First, as already noted, little of the research and few of the policy prescriptions have anything to say about the cost-effectiveness of various proposed interventions. Knowledge of the factors that affect learning, and hence important policy prescriptions, do exist. But these have not been ranked in terms of potential cost-effectiveness based on Peruvian research. It would be a time-consuming task, though not scientifically demanding, to carry out some type of meta-analysis of the various "production function" studies that have been done, attach benefits to the impacts, assess the cost of the proposed changes, and propose some prioritization.

Second, few of the studies focus on the management and institutional economic issues that will have to be resolved if the problems are to be confronted. That is, most of the "production function" studies identified above (including our own analysis of the 2001 national evaluation results) tend to identify the "what" issues. However, there is little analysis of the managerial and policy issues that are blocking action on the "what" issues, which is particularly disturbing if those "what" issues appear so clear. The "how" is relatively under-researched, though a few analysts such as Hunt (2001) have looked into the issue. As background for this report, some research on institutional management or "how" issues was done at the school or classroom level. This area of work needs to be further developed in Peru, though it is not clear that a whole new industry, similar to that which has emerged on the "what" issues, needs to develop. A few well-done studies at two levels (classroom and school, and system) will go a long way.

Third, there are few truly successful and well-evaluated experiments that put the key policy recommendations to work and show unmistakable, large-scale, systemic improvements in learning achievement. It is known that there are schools that produce good results even though their clientele is poor. There have been a few donor or NGO projects that have produced improved results in a few schools. However, few (none that could be found for this report) projects have had large measured impacts on student achievement in a whole system or sub-system (a whole district or province). Thus, there are few credible models of *systemic interventions* that truly work in driving cognitive development among the poor.

The most significant problem that remains is coming to clear policy agreements on the determinants of learning and implementing solutions over an extended period. Coming to agreement on standards, management, accountability, and the needed spending, and then developing stable management teams (from the Ministerial level down to the school principal level) to lead the implementation effort over many years, appears to be, thus far, less attainable than producing knowledge. The following chapter suggests some reasons for these kinds of failures.

CHAPTER 3

The Accountability-Triangle Approach

Previous chapters have explained that at this point in time, Peru's main problem in the education sector is quality, and more specifically, providing quality education to the poor. Chapter 2 also noted that there is no shortage of technical suggestions and solutions. It seems, therefore, that the problems that remain are problems of "political will", or accountability. This report takes as its point of departure an accountability framework that proposes that for any social system (education in this case) to work well there has to be a well-defined and well-exercised framework of mutual accountabilities between three (or four, depending on how one counts) sets of actors, as set out in Figure 3.1. The figure is sometimes referred to as "the accountability triangle." The accountability framework used in this section is an elaboration of the framework used in various recent World Bank reports (see Fiszbein 2004; World Bank 2003).

The three key sets of actors are: a) the State (including its regional or subnational manifestations), which includes politicians and policymakers in both the legislative and executive branches, b) the service providers (which could be subdivided further into organizations such the ministerial bureaucracy, regional bureaucracies such as DREs and UGELs), and the actual service providers such as schools, and c) the citizens or clients of the system.

The relationships between political actors and service providers (the right leg of the triangle) are often referred to as "compact". The relationships at the base of the triangle are relationships of "local participation," "local voice," or "consumer choice." And the relationships in the left leg of the triangle are called "voice" relationships. (Sometimes "national" or "aggregated" voice to distinguish it from the participatory voice relationship at the base of the triangle.)

In Peru, many of these relationships work imperfectly at best, and in some cases hardly work at all, as the rest of this report and other reports in the RECURSO series document. Due to lack of space and time, two relationships are emphasized in this report: the bottom

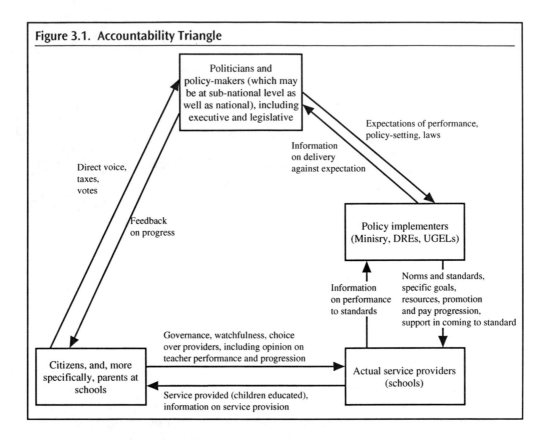

Figure 3.1. Accountability Triangle

of the triangle, and the right side of the triangle. Voice issues, those on the left hand side of the triangle, are covered, but more lightly. In any case, the rest of this report does not focus on taking each side of the triangle in turn; in fact, the report is not organized specifically around the triangle. Instead, the various issues are treated in more traditionally "topical" chapters. For example, "compact" issues having to do with funding and with standards are dealt with in Chapter 4 and in Chapter 6; issues of accountability to parents and community are dealt with in Chapter 7, Chapter 8 and more explicitly in Chapter 9; and so forth.

Education Finance

Patterns of Educational Expenditure

Financing of the education sector, and of schools in general, is a key part of the "compact" between the state's politicians, policymakers, and service providers. Previous sections have explored the provision of education services, noting that Peru has done very well in providing widespread access to education. It has been noted here that while Peru's average level of quality provision is not much below what one would expect, the quality of provision is nonetheless much lower than that of countries with which Peru would like to compete. Furthermore, it has been argued that there is a gap between mass access and the quality of that access: the ratio of access to quality is higher than the international average. Finally, it has also been noted that there is a problem with the fact that quality is highly variable particularly given its relatively (though not unexpectedly) low level. The predictability of learning outcomes, particularly among the poor, is very low, even considering their poverty. This section and the next suggests that there is something to the spending patterns—and the management of that spending—that helps account for these results. This section looks at the patterns of expenditure by type of expenditure, and the next section focuses on patterns of expenditure by the income level and socioeconomic status of the recipients.

In discussing spending patterns, it is useful to have some "macro" or systemic benchmarks or goals. These are not easily established in the abstract or via reference only to local studies; international comparisons are most useful in this case. Table 4.1 sets out some international benchmarks for the key expenditure parameters. Two types of benchmarks are used. First, the average for Latin America as a whole is presented. This is useful, but since Latin America as a whole is not necessarily a set of countries to be emulated, a set of three Latin American countries (Chile, Cuba, and Mexico) with the best performances in Latin American in the PISA or LLECE assessments is selected for comparison. Finally, a set

Table 4.1. Calculation of Expenditure Benchmarks Suitable for Peru

Comparison Point	Primary Expenditure Per Pupil/GDP Per Capita	Year	Secondary Expenditure Per Pupil/GDP Per Capita	Year	Tertiary Expenditure Per Student/GDP Per Capita	Year	Source for Previous Three Columns	Current Expenditure/Total Expenditure	Years	Source	Personnel/Total Cost	Trend from 1970s to 1990s	Year	Source for Benchmark	Source for Trend
Latin America total	12%	Most recent for each country	15%	Most recent for each country	44%	Most recent possible for each country	EDSTATS	87% recently, 92% historically	1970s to 2001	1	70%	−0.4 percentage points/ year	Projected 2001	8	16
Chile	14%	2000	15%	2000	19%	2000	EDSTATS	85% recently, 94% historically	1970s to 2001	2	52%	−0.3 percentage points/ year	2001	9	17
Cuba	33%	2000	43%	2000	96%	2000	EDSTATS	NA			53%	0.6 percentage points/ year	2002	10	18
Mexico	12%	1999	14%	1999	45%	1999	EDSTATS	97% recently, 71% historically	1970s to 2001	3	88%	NA	2001	11	
Average of above three	20%		24%		53%						64%				
Finland	22%	1996	26%	1996	43%	1996	EDSTATS	92%	1970s to 2001	4	59%	0.2 percentage points/ year	2001	12	19
Korea	18%	2000	17%	2000	8%	2000	EDSTATS	79%	1970s to 2001	5	55%	−0.8 percentage points/ year	2001	13	20
United Kingdom	14%	2000	13%	2000	32%	2000	EDSTATS	93%	1970s to 2001	6	66%	−2 percentage points/ year	2001	14	21
Thailand	17%	1999	15%	1999	26%	1999	EDSTATS	82%	1970s to 2001	7	72%	−0.3 percentage points/ year	Projected 2001	15	22

Average of above four	18%	18%	27%	87%	63%	
Appropriate approximate benchmark or goal for Peru	16%	16%	31%	87%–89%	65%–70%	−0.2 to −0.3 per-centage points/ year

Sources:

1 Calculated and projected from IMF data sourced from EDSTATS at http://sima.worldbank.org/edstats/drbe.asp and for historical series, UNESCO at http://www.uis.unesco.org/pagesen/DBExpTCC.asp

2 Calculated from http://www.oecd.org/dataoecd/62/17/33671056.xls and http://www.oecd.org/dataoecd/62/20/33670986.xls and for historical series, UNESCO at http://www.uis.unesco.org/pagesen/DBExpTCC.asp

3 Calculated from http://www.oecd.org/dataoecd/62/17/33671056.xls and http://www.oecd.org/dataoecd/62/20/33670986.xls and for historical series, UNESCO at http://www.uis.unesco.org/pagesen/DBExpTCC.asp

4 Calculated and projected from http://www.oecd.org/dataoecd/62/17/33671056.xls and http://www.oecd.org/dataoecd/62/20/33670986.xls and for historical series, UNESCO at http://www.uis.unesco.org/pagesen/DBExpTCC.asp

5 Calculated and projected from http://www.oecd.org/dataoecd/62/17/33671056.xls and http://www.oecd.org/dataoecd/62/20/33670986.xls and for historical series, UNESCO at http://www.uis.unesco.org/pagesen/DBExpTCC.asp

6 Calculated and projected from http://www.oecd.org/dataoecd/62/17/33671056.xls and http://www.oecd.org/dataoecd/62/20/33670986.xls and for historical series, UNESCO at http://www.uis.unesco.org/pagesen/DBExpTCC.asp

7 Calculated and projected from IMF data sourced from EDSTATS at http://sima.worldbank.org/edstats/drbe.asp and for historical series, UNESCO at http://www.uis.unesco.org/pagesen/DBExpTCC.asp

8 Calculated from UNESCO historical data at http://www.uis.unesco.org/pagesen/DBExpLevel.asp and http://www.uis.unesco.org/pagesen/DBExpPurpose.asp

9 Calculated from http://www.oecd.org/dataoecd/62/17/33671056.xls and http://www.oecd.org/dataoecd/62/20/33670986.xls

10 Ministry of Finance http://www.mfp.cu/educacion.htm

11 Calculated from http://www.oecd.org/dataoecd/62/17/33671056.xls and http://www.oecd.org/dataoecd/62/20/33670986.xls

12 Calculated from http://www.oecd.org/dataoecd/62/17/33671056.xls and http://www.oecd.org/dataoecd/62/20/33670986.xls

13 Calculated and projected from http://www.oecd.org/dataoecd/62/17/33671056.xls and http://www.oecd.org/dataoecd/62/20/33670986.xls

14 Calculated from http://www.oecd.org/dataoecd/62/17/33671056.xls and http://www.oecd.org/dataoecd/62/20/33670986.xls

15 Calculated from UNESCO historical data at http://www.uis.unesco.org/pagesen/DBExpLevel.asp and http://www.uis.unesco.org/pagesen/DBExpPurpose.asp

16 Calculated from UNESCO historical data at http://www.uis.unesco.org/pagesen/DBExpLevel.asp and http://www.uis.unesco.org/pagesen/DBExpPurpose.asp

17 Calculated from UNESCO historical data at http://www.uis.unesco.org/pagesen/DBExpLevel.asp and http://www.uis.unesco.org/pagesen/DBExpPurpose.asp plus OECD http://www.oecd.org/dataoecd/62/17/33671056.xls and http://www.oecd.org/dataoecd/62/20/33670986.xls

18 Calculated from UNESCO historical data at http://www.uis.unesco.org/pagesen/DBExpLevel.asp and http://www.uis.unesco.org/pagesen/DBExpPurpose.asp plus OECD http://www.oecd.org/dataoecd/62/17/33671056.xls and http://www.oecd.org/dataoecd/62/20/33670986.xls

19 Calculated from UNESCO historical data at http://www.uis.unesco.org/pagesen/DBExpLevel.asp and http://www.uis.unesco.org/pagesen/DBExpPurpose.asp plus OECD http://www.oecd.org/dataoecd/62/17/33671056.xls and http://www.oecd.org/dataoecd/62/20/33670986.xls

20 Calculated from UNESCO historical data at http://www.uis.unesco.org/pagesen/DBExpLevel.asp and http://www.uis.unesco.org/pagesen/DBExpPurpose.asp plus OECD http://www.oecd.org/dataoecd/62/17/33671056.xls and http://www.oecd.org/dataoecd/62/20/33670986.xls

21 Calculated from UNESCO historical data at http://www.uis.unesco.org/pagesen/DBExpLevel.asp and http://www.uis.unesco.org/pagesen/DBExpPurpose.asp plus OECD http://www.oecd.org/dataoecd/62/17/33671056.xls and http://www.oecd.org/dataoecd/62/20/33670986.xls

22 Calculated from UNESCO historical data at http://www.uis.unesco.org/pagesen/DBExpLevel.asp and http://www.uis.unesco.org/pagesen/DBExpPurpose.asp

of countries from elsewhere in the world is chosen. This set contains a variety of situations. Two (the United Kingdom and Finland) are developed countries with good educational performance. One, Korea, recently gained status as a largely developed country, and is known to have placed a great deal of emphasis on education. Another, Thailand, is still a developing country, but its educational performance has improved significantly in the last few decades and it performs well on international comparisons.

This set of countries provides some parameters for some of the key spending proportions to be discussed below:

1. The proportion of personnel expenditure to total (current and capital) expenditure. This is a remarkably firm parameter across the comparators proposed, and a reasonable goal or benchmark for a system ought to be in the range of 65 to 70 percent. (This assumes the payout of pensions to retired teachers and administrators is not counted as expenditure of the education sector itself.)

2. Most importantly, countries that appear to be making substantial progress have decreased this proportion over time, at a rate that suggests a benchmark of some 0.2 to 0.3 percentage points per year. An interesting exception is Cuba, which increased the proportion of total expenditure devoted to personnel, but note that this increase came from an extremely low proportion of around 40 percent.

3. The proportion of current expenditure to total expenditure. This is a somewhat more variable parameter, but a benchmark of 87 to 89 percent appears recommendable. The values for already highly-developed societies such as the United Kingdom and Finland seem less relevant in this case, because these societies do not need to engage in as much infrastructure expansion as Peru does, or as Peru has had to in the recent past.

4. Per pupil spending on primary, secondary, and tertiary education as a proportion of GDP per capita are useful benchmarks not only of adequacy but also of balance between the sub-sectors. These benchmarks are proposed at around 14, 17, and 40 percent of GDP per capita, noting the approximately 3 to 1 ratio between tertiary, on the one hand, and primary and secondary expenditure per student, on the other. The percentage spent on each sub-sector (without taking into account enrollment, and without reference to GDP per capita) is not as useful a benchmark, because it depends so much on enrollment patterns. (The optimality of enrollment patterns is a different matter and can be benchmarked.)

5. Finally, note that public spending on education as a percentage of GDP is not explicitly benchmarked, but its level in Peru is analyzed below.

Education System Efficiency

As noted, Peru spends about 3 percent of its GDP to support education through public expenditure. This proportion is not benchmarked, as its value is relatively meaningless without reference to what is "produced" in exchange for the expenditure. Figure 4.1 provides a graphic analysis of what is "produced", in terms of enrollment, with this public expenditure.

Table 4.2 below shows the allocation of resources for Peru by input or item as well as by sub-sector. The share of the total expenditure to GDP, as well as per student expenditure

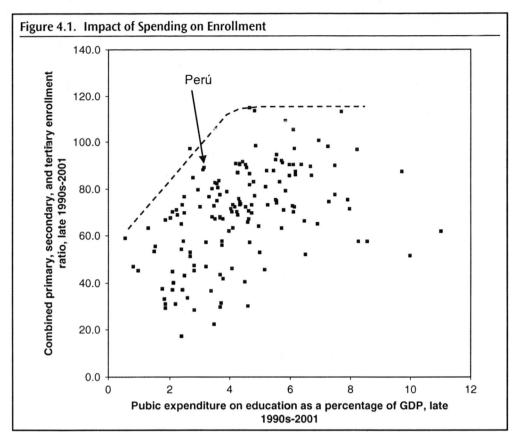

Figure 4.1. Impact of Spending on Enrollment

Sources: Graphed from EDSTATS data.

as a proportion of GDP, is also shown. This table captures the essence of the spending patterns to be analyzed. From these data, and from a comparison against key benchmarks noted above, a few facts stand out:

1. Personnel expenditure is much too high and, even worse, is going in the wrong direction. A reasonable goal or benchmark is somewhere in the range of 65 to 70 percent, but Peru is now at 75 percent. A goal should be to reduce this by some 0.3 percentage points per year, as soon as possible.
2. Partly because of this, total current expenditure is going up as well, from 86 percent of total expenditure a few years ago to 93 percent in 2004 and 90 percent in 2005. A goal should be to come back down to 86 percent as soon as possible.
3. The ratios of spending per student as a proportion of GDP per capita are fairly low, but the proportions among these ratios are approximately right.
4. Education expenditure as a proportion of GDP is essentially static at about 3 percent of GDP. If one were to add expenditure on pensions of retired employees, this proportion would increase, but this practice is not common in other countries. The share of public education expenditure on GDP is not explicitly benchmarked. Instead, a comparative analysis is carried out below.

Table 4.2. Key Expenditure Patterns in Peru

Executed expenditure by in current soles	1999	2000	2001	2002	2003	2004	2005
Pre-primary	455,362,385	447,844,586	424,879,367	511,391,632	552,244,738	577,005,100	591,656,097
Primary	1,908,927,546	1,954,677,866	1,858,705,124	2,027,035,600	2,177,134,136	2,508,777,484	2,581,453,819
Secondary	1,307,764,908	1,400,018,509	1,453,401,116	1,657,277,423	1,822,417,565	2,146,553,419	2,330,576,939
Post-secondary	910,965,662	952,391,760	961,446,990	1,042,729,074	1,165,158,687	1,341,661,558	1,453,697,980
Others	587,758,159	602,581,653	696,310,071	756,058,920	867,134,251	913,605,108	1,057,625,248
Total	5,170,778,661	5,357,514,373	5,394,742,667	5,994,492,649	6,584,089,378	7,487,602,670	8,015,010,084

Numbers of students in public institutions	1999	2000	2001	2002	2003	2004	2005
Pre-primary	899,625	929,400	934,150	937,846	913,257	922,379	919,369
Primary	3,795,118	3,761,516	3,725,495	3,683,949	3,627,104	3,571,721	3,589,997
Secondary	1,913,790	1,972,424	2,057,807	2,099,412	2,106,977	2,142,044	2,130,472
Post-secondary	531,491	556,725	554,131	583,979	601,209	589,570	593,411
Total	7,140,024	7,220,065	7,271,583	7,305,186	7,248,547	7,225,714	7,233,249

Nominal expenditure per student, current soles	1999	2000	2001	2002	2003	2004	2005
Pre-primary	506	482	455	545	605	626	644
Primary	503	520	499	550	600	702	719
Secondary	683	710	706	789	865	1,002	1,094
Post-secondary	1,714	1,711	1,735	1,786	1,938	2,276	2,450

Expenditure per capita as percentage of GDP per capita	1999	2000	2001	2002	2003	2004	2005
Pre-primary	7.4%	6.7%	6.4%	7.3%	7.8%	7.4%	7.1%
Primary	7.4%	7.3%	7.0%	7.4%	7.7%	8.3%	7.9%
Secondary	10.0%	9.9%	9.9%	10.6%	11.1%	11.8%	12.0%
Post-secondary	25.2%	23.9%	24.3%	24.0%	24.9%	26.8%	26.9%

Executed expenditure, by item, current soles	1999	2000	2001	2002	2003	2004	2005
Wages and Salaries	3,668,638,604	3,875,095,524	4,047,762,965	4,619,170,622	5,016,534,904	5,534,229,011	6,027,665,971
Goods and Services	684,779,282	769,227,072	816,852,375	830,727,653	890,734,279	992,464,713	988,000,869

	1999	2000	2001	2002	2003	2004	2005
Other Current Expenditures	104,303,674	110,369,944	113,102,198	136,795,539	207,623,147	427,319,637	166,592,942
Total Current Expenditure	4,457,721,560	4,754,692,539	4,977,717,537	5,586,693,814	6,114,892,330	6,954,013,360	7,182,259,782
Investment	644,191,083	527,186,228	346,866,719	334,004,558	350,149,572	389,782,653	645,221,065
Financial investment	10,549,462	13,015,401	14,417,068	12,247,522	20,031,363	20,989,688	14,769,305
Debt amortization	0	277,804	861,240	1,923,213	724,661	988,506	1,065,033
Interests repayment	864,134	768,942	1,122,557	890,343	543,446	355,445	132,670
Other Capital Expenditures	57,452,423	61,573,458	53,757,546	58,733,200	97,748,005	121,473,017	171,562,228
Total Capital Expenditure	713,057,102	602,821,834	417,025,130	407,798,835	469,197,048	533,589,309	832,750,301
Grand Total	5,170,778,661	5,357,514,373	5,394,742,667	5,994,492,649	6,584,089,378	7,487,602,670	8,015,010,084

Key ratios	1999	2000	2001	2002	2003	2004	2005
Wages and salaries expenditure as a percentage of total expenditure	71%	72%	75%	77%	76%	74%	75%
Current expenditure as percentage of total expenditure	86%	89%	92%	93%	93%	93%	90%
Total public education expenditure as percentage of GDP	3.0%	2.9%	2.9%	3.0%	3.1%	3.2%	3.2%

Rates of growth	1999–2005
Nominal salary spending	8.6%
Current spending	8.3%
Total spending	7.6%
CPI	2.5%
Total enrollment	0.2%
Real salary spending per student	6.0%
Real current spending per student	5.6%
Real total spending per student	4.7%

Source: SIAF and *Ministerio de Educación, Cifras de la Educación 1998–2004.*
GDP: Central Bank and INEI, http://www.bcrp.gob.pe/Espanol/WEstadistica/cuadros/mensuales/Nota_2000/ncua_052.xls
Population: INEI projections.
1. Only functional expenditure

In more general terms, aside from the issue of benchmarks, it should be noted that growth in spending in Peru is now almost totally driven by growth in spending per student as opposed to growth in enrollment. Enrollment is growing at only 0.2 percent per year, yet total real expenditure is growing at 5.0 percent per year (7.6 percent nominal growth minus 2.5 percent inflation). And this is largely driven by salary pressure. Salary cost growth is the driver in the system and, as will be seen, is in turn partly driven by decreases in the pupil-teacher ratio below levels that appear justified, but mostly driven by increases in salary levels.

Figure 4.1 shows a freehand curve that depicts the approximate "limit" of production possibilities as derived from a simple cross-national analysis. It shows Peru to be fairly close to this "frontier." In other words, Peru has been a fairly efficient producer of enrollment or coverage. A more formal analysis carried out by Herrera and Pang took, as input variables, per capita expenditure in primary and secondary education and, as output variables, the net primary and secondary enrollment rates, average years of education, primary and secondary completion rates, and the literacy rate. According to their results, Peru does relatively well with respect to other countries. In short, Peru's institutions know how to turn resources into enrollment, and do it quite well.

This is not the case for quality, however. Peru is not an efficient spender on quality or learning. Thus, it is unlikely that quality could be efficiently improved simply by spending more, by buying more inputs—expenditure and resources do not appear to be the binding constraint to further improvements in learning, based either on macro analysis as shown in Figure 4.2 (below) or on the micro analysis previously shown in Chapter 2.

This analysis suggests that Peru is about 30 percent away from the central trend, or that its inefficiency in producing learning achievement is about 30 percent. More detailed analysis of the efficiency with which learning is produced, using not international comparison but micro data (from the 2001 National Assessment) from Peru itself, shows similar results.[9] A micro analysis by school level was done for this study taking as an output variable the average score in Spanish ("comunicación integral") and Mathematics ("lógico-matemática") and as input variables those that were the most significant in the estimation of the production function.[10] For primary education, the inefficiency level is 25 percent. In other words, in terms of learning results, the primary education sector could perhaps produce as much as 25 percent more under the same socioeconomic conditions it already faces and the same level of inputs as currently used, if management were tighter and the system could produce to standard.

---

9. The work of Pablo Lavado in this section is acknowledged with gratitude.

10. The estimate of the frontier was based on classical Data Envelope Analysis (DEA). This type of analysis is not robust to outliers—on the contrary, it is highly sensitive to outliers. (However, it has certain advantages that warrant its use.) Outliers could be due to poor data, or to practices that are truly non-replicable by other schools or "production units." Thus how outliers are dealt with seems important. Our judgment was that practices that result in efficiency levels greater than two standard deviations from the mean were likely non-replicable and invalid as a way of estimating the average inefficiency of the rest of the observations. In order to establish this, we: 1) carried out several OLS estimates of the impact of each of the input on each of the output variables; 2) took the each observation's residual, for each one of the regressions, and compared them to the standard deviation of the residuals for that regression; and 3) finally, we excluded those observations which showed a residual greater than two standard deviations on any regression. In the analysis, the vertical axis is the combination of mathematics and Spanish results, and the horizontal axis is an index of a combination of inputs and socioeconomic conditions.

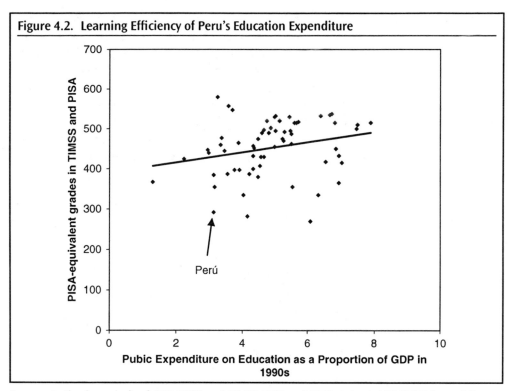

Figure 4.2. Learning Efficiency of Peru's Education Expenditure

Source: Author's analysis of PISA 2000 and TIMSS 1999 and 2003 data and EDSTATS for public expenditure data.

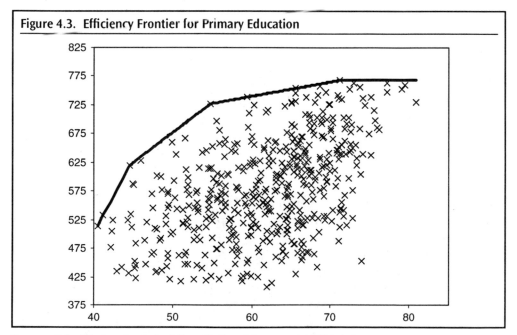

Figure 4.3. Efficiency Frontier for Primary Education

Source: Calculated and graphed from National Assessment 2001 data.

In secondary education, the inefficiency level is only 8.4 percent. Note, in particular, the fact that a lot of schools are bunched along the efficiency frontier towards the lower end of the horizontal axis. Why secondary education appears more efficient is unknown. Perhaps the fact that there are fewer schools makes it easier to apply standards and provide some supervision. Perhaps the inputs are better in some way that is difficult to measure and thus schools simply appear more efficient, but in reality have better—or, at any rate, more uniform—inputs. Also, it may be that as the harder-to-teach children have already dropped out, the secondary system simply appears more efficient. The children who remain at school are those whose scores are higher and show less dispersion.

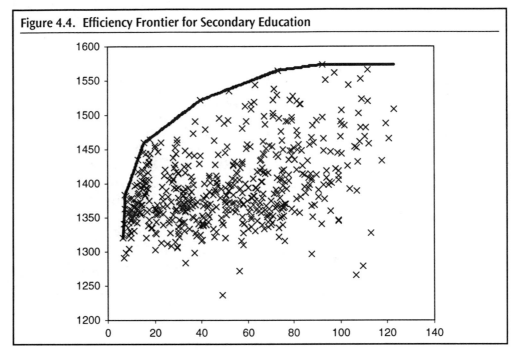

Figure 4.4. Efficiency Frontier for Secondary Education

Source: Calculated and graphed from National Assessment 2001 data.

All of these results are both related to and echo those obtained in the estimation of the production function for this report, as well as the results of other researchers (both reported in Chapter 2). The wide dispersion of results, particularly among the poor, is the result of: a) poor management and standards, and this affects the poor in particular, as well as b) the fact that the poor are not only (obviously) poorer, but face a greater dispersion of other factors associated with poverty: not all the poor are equally malnourished, and not all the poor are equally less likely to speak Spanish at home than the well-off.

Many in Peru advocate for increased expenditure on education. In fact, in some lists of policy proposals this is the only fixed, quantitative goal. But things are not so simple, as has just been shown. It is true that Peru is an efficient spender on coverage or access. Yet, Chapter 2 has shown that quality is much more of a constraint to advancement in Peru than access is. Second, Chapters 2 and 4 show, that there is no apparent strong relationship between spending and quality in Peru at either the macro or school level. As has been noted above, costs from salaries and personnel-related benefits are squeezing the budget. Yet, lower pupil-teacher ratios in Peru are not associated with increased learning. Thus, a great deal of expenditure is accounted for by the provision of teachers in a manner that does not seem to make much difference to achievement levels. For all these reasons, and as discussed in the Policy Recommendations, this report advocates that before there is much more expenditure on the sector, the sector needs to take administrative measures that put it closer to the efficiency frontier in terms of learning.

Spending Incidence and Equity

Incidence of Public Expenditure by Income Group

Elsewhere in this report (Chapter 1) it has been noted that Peru's worst performing learners perform much worse than the worst-performing learners of other middle-income countries participating in PISA 2000; additionally, they perform much worse, relatively speaking, than Peru's best-performing students. It is also shown, in Chapter 2, that this poor performance is strongly associated with, though not entirely determined by, the poverty of students' families. Another possible cause of particularly poor results among the poor could be that education inputs are distributed so as not to favor the poor. In any case, education spending represents an important public benefit and is a significant source of current transfers to the poor; as such, its distribution is a fundamental issue. This section explores the incidence of spending across income groupings.

Public spending on education, in the basic levels, is favorable to the poor, as shown by the data in Table 4.3 and in Table 4.4. The poor (the first two quintiles) benefit more than other groups from public spending (see Total row), but particularly benefit in the basic levels (pre-primary, primary, and secondary). The data on benefits shown below have been calculated first assuming equal expenditure per beneficiary across quintiles (Table 4.3), and then using per capita spending levels that vary by *Departamento,* which are then mapped to quintiles (Table 4.4).[11] The former is therefore simply equivalent to the distribution of beneficiaries of public education by quintile. Presenting the data in this manner (one version assuming equal per capita expenditure across quintiles, the other assuming varying per capita expenditure) is relatively uncommon in these sorts of calculations. Most benefit-incidence calculations for other countries assume equal spending per pupil and are thus really a calculation of beneficiary incidence, not of benefit incidence. If spending per student—even within the public sector—is negatively correlated with the poverty of students, then this traditional incidence analysis over-states the progressiveness of spending. We can see from Table 4.3 and Table 4.4 that, using either definition, public education spending in Peru appears quite pro-poor compared with spending in other countries (data for other countries shown in Table 4.5). Naturally, the data on actual benefit incidence

---

11. This is possible because data on per student spending disaggregated by *Departamento* are available, and each family in the ENAHO 2003 (Fourth Quarter) can be associated with a *Departamento.* This implicitly assumes that every family in the *Departamento* receives the *Departamento*-wide per student spending. This is clearly a simplification, but it is better than assuming nation-wide equality of per student spending.

Table 4.3. Beneficiary Incidence by Quintile, 2003 (assuming *equal* spending per beneficiary)

Education Level	Income quintiles grouped by household income				
	I	II	III	IV	V
Pre-Primary	24.3%	22.5%	24.2%	19.3%	9.8%
Primary	33.4%	27.2%	21.0%	13.3%	5.1%
Secondary	19.4%	24.4%	27.1%	20.3%	8.9%
Non univ. tertiary	4.5%	19.2%	31.2%	27.2%	17.9%
Undergraduate university	1.4%	4.7%	13.5%	33.5%	46.8%
Graduate	0.0%	0.0%	0.0%	15.2%	84.8%
Total post-secondary	2.6%	10.1%	19.9%	30.7%	36.7%
Total	25.8%	24.5%	23.1%	17.4%	9.2%

Sources: Beneficiaries: ENAHO 2003-IV Term; Pre-tertiary Benefits: Public Budget National Bureau, Ministry of Economics and Finance. Tertiary Benefits: *Sistema Integrado de Administración Financiera,* Ministry of Economics and Finance.

Table 4.4. Benefit Incidence by Quintile, 2003 (assuming *unequal* spending per beneficiary)

Education Level	Income quintiles grouped by household income				
	I	II	III	IV	V
Pre-Primary	19.6%	20.9%	25.6%	23.7%	10.2%
Primary	31.8%	26.8%	21.9%	14.0%	5.5%
Secondary	18.2%	24.1%	27.3%	20.8%	9.5%
Non univ. tertiary	3.7%	16.5%	33.3%	27.5%	19.0%
Undergraduate university	1.1%	5.5%	13.4%	31.3%	48.7%
Graduate	0.0%	0.0%	0.0%	16.9%	83.1%
Total post-secondary	1.6%	7.4%	16.8%	30.1%	44.1%
Total	19.4%	20.9%	22.7%	20.7%	16.2%

Sources: Beneficiaries: Computed from ENAHO 2003-IV Term; Pre-tertiary Benefits: Public Budget National Bureau, Ministry of Economics and Finance. Tertiary Benefits: *Sistema Integrado de Administración Financiera,* Ministry of Economics and Finance.

Table 4.5. Benefit or Beneficiary Incidence—International Medians in Various Years[12]

Education Level	Income quintiles				
	I	II	III	IV	V
Primary	20.7%	22.8%	21.3%	20.2%	15.0%
Secondary	10.7%	16.1%	20.6%	24.5%	28.1%
Tertiary	3.5%	7.4%	14.8%	25.2%	49.1%
Total	14.7%	17.5%	19.6%	21.4%	26.8%

Source: Calculated from EDSTATS data.

---

12. Because the original medians calculated from the data do not add up to 100 percent, even though the underlying data do, the medians have been re-normed to add up to 100 percent. The deviation of the sums of medians across quintiles from 100 percent was usually only one or two percent, thus re-norming does not change things very much. Countries included in the sample are: Armenia, Côte d'Ivoire, Ecuador, Ghana, Guinea, Guyana, Indonesia, Jamaica, Kazakhstan, Kenya, Kyrgyz Republic, Madagascar, Malawi, Morocco, Nepal, Nicaragua, Pakistan, Panama, Peru 1994, Romania, South Africa, Tanzania, Uganda, Uruguay, and Vietnam.

(Table 4.3), as opposed to beneficiary incidence (Table 4.4), shows less progressiveness because per pupil spending in poor *Departamentos* is lower than spending in the richer *Departamentos.*

However, because education is not a targeted program, the poor's disproportionately large benefit (that is, the progressiveness of education spending) is largely a matter of default, as the better-off have fewer children and also self-select out of the public system.[13] The progressiveness of public spending on education is not the result of either active policy choice or management. Primary education serves as an example. The poorest quintile receives a proportion of the public spending which is 6 times higher than that received by the richest quintile (30 percent as opposed to 5 percent, approximately—see Table 4.4). But, as shown in Table 4.6, this is because families in the richest quintile have one third as many children of primary school age as the families in the poorest quintile, and because one half of them choose to send their children to private schools, whereas essentially none of the poorest attend private school. In general, the apparent progressiveness of public allocation to education is determined by three factors: the degree to which the poor have more children than the rich, the degree to which they choose or are able to enroll them in school, and the degree to which they choose or are able to enroll them in private schools. (It should be noted that the proportion of the overall population attending private schools is about the same in Peru as in the rest of Latin America, or perhaps slightly less at the secondary level.) The impact of these three types of determinants is analyzed below, starting with the proportion of youths who attend school by income quintile.

Table 4.6. Demographic and Public Private Choice of Families, by Income Quintile, as Determinants of Pro-poor Spending, 2003

School Level	Numbers of children per household in the appropriate age groups		Proportion of children attending private schooling	
	Income quintiles		Income quintiles	
	I	V	I	V
Pre-primary	0.4[14]	0.2	0%	60%
Primary	0.9	0.3	1%	49%
Secondary	0.7	0.3	2%	51%
Post-secondary	0.4	0.5	0%	60%
Total	2.4	1.3	1%	55%

Source: Computed from ENAHO 2003-IV Term.

---

13. In one important sense the fact that the benefits of primary education are distributed in a more progressive manner than the benefits of secondary education is a result of policy, namely the policy of ensuring universal coverage first at the primary level and placing more primary than secondary schools in rural locations. However, this fact does little to explain why spending on primary education is so pro-poor—this has more to do with private choice than with public policy.

14. There are some anomalies in this table that require further research. For example, it is not clear why quintile V households would have half as many children per household of secondary school age as quintile-I households, but more children of post-secondary school age than quintile-I families. The possibility that this could be the result of the definition of household, and the possibility that older children may be working, may form their own households and may have higher per person income than that of the family from which they originated was investigated but the hypothesis was rejected.

Table 4.7. Proportion of Youths Enrolled in School 2003[15]

Education level	Income quintiles grouped by household income				
	I	II	III	IV	V
Pre-Primary	0.37	0.46	0.59	0.74	0.81
Primary	1.14	1.14	1.03	1.05	0.99
Secondary	0.54	0.77	1.02	1.01	0.99
Post-secondary	0.03	0.15	0.28	0.47	0.87
Total	0.66	0.73	0.78	0.82	0.92

Source: Computed from ENAHO 2003-IV Term.

It is clear then that one of the main reasons why, say, the distribution of secondary schooling expenditure is not as progressive as that of primary spending is that poorer families choose, or are able, to send their children to secondary school only about half as frequently as rich families.

The other two components, or determinants of progressiveness, are presented in Table 4.6. As noted, at the primary level, the rich have about one third as many children per household as the poor; the propensity of the rich to send their children to school is the same as that of the poor, but half of the rich children attend private schooling. Thus, rich families' benefit from public spending is only one-sixth as high as the benefit received by the poor. At the secondary level spending is not nearly as favorable to the poor, largely because the poor enroll with only one half the frequency attributable to the rich.

Thus, in effect, the relatively pro-poor nature of public spending on basic education is somewhat of an illusion. This may result in policy "surprises." One policy "surprise" that could arise is that, if the quality of public education were to improve, public schooling would tend to automatically become less favorable to the poor, as the relatively better-off would tend to opt back into public schooling. If quality improved strictly through policy changes, rather than through increases in per student spending, the fact that the public sector would suddenly have more clients, and more of them would be well off, would mean that costs would go up, and these costs would be less pro-poor. If the increases in quality also required increases in per student spending, the fiscal impact would be greater. It may be thought that fiscal pressure of this nature could simply be resisted. But greater upper-middle class participation in public schooling (if the quality of public schooling were to increase) would tend to mean more public support for public spending on education, as the upper middle class speaks with a disproportionate voice. This is hardly an argument against increasing the quality of public education. Yet, it does suggest that it is odd to consider current spending patterns to be pro-poor in any really meaningful sense.

The notion that public spending benefits the poor disproportionately as a result of private choices, rather than because of policy decisions, suggests a need to analyze spending within the public sector in more detail. This analysis is carried out below, after the relative incidence of spending has been analyzed.

---

15. The proportions can be greater than one because the denominator refers to children in the appropriate age group, whereas the numerator refers to all children. This keeps the data consistent with the gross enrollment ratio data presented in the section on outcomes elsewhere in this report.

The public transfers to poor families that are implicit in access to public education are very large. Table 4.8 shows the size of the transfer, by income quintile, relative to total family consumption. The size of the total transfers to all families in each income quintile is shown relative to the total consumption of all households in those quintiles, not simply those with children in public schools.

Table 4.8.   Benefits Represented by Public School Subsidy as a Proportion of Total Household Expenditure Across All Households ("Relative Incidence"), 2003

Education level	Income quintiles				
	I	II	III	IV	V
Pre-Primary	1.9%	1.1%	0.9%	0.6%	0.1%
Primary	14.5%	6.8%	3.8%	1.7%	0.3%
Secondary	7.1%	5.2%	4.0%	2.1%	0.4%
Total tertiary	0.5%	1.2%	1.8%	2.3%	1.4%
Total	24.0%	14.3%	10.6%	6.6%	2.2%

Sources: Beneficiaries: ENAHO 2003-IV Term; Pre-tertiary Benefits: Public Budget National Bureau, Ministry of Economics and Finance. Tertiary Benefits: *Sistema Integrado de Administración Financiera,* Ministry of Economics and Finance.

Two points in particular are worth noting in Table 4.8. The impact of primary school subsidies on the poorest households is very large. Education thus probably represents the most significant in-kind subsidy for the poor—perhaps more important than any other type of public spending. The fact that education represents such a large transfer to the poor highlights the importance of "getting management right." If this transfer is under-delivering actual education and learning to the poor, relative to its potential and its cost, then the waste of both this potential and cost is very large.

The high degree of benefit to the poor relative to their total expenditure is a product of two facts: first, that public spending on education is very large relative to any other form of expenditure and to total national income (compared to other social expenditure in Peru, not compared to the same ratio in other countries), and second, that at the primary level this expenditure is so disproportionately (six to one) favorably distributed to the poor.

A second important point to note in Table 4.8 is that though the richest quintile captures the largest proportion of the subsidy represented by tertiary education (as shown in Table 4.4), the *relative* importance of this subsidy is highest for quintile IV and is actually higher for quintile III than for quintile V. In this sense, the higher education subsidy is more of a middle-class (in the quantitative sense of being in the middle, not in the sociological sense of having a "modern" lifestyle and level of consumption) subsidy than a rich-family subsidy. This is the result of three factors. First, the probability that a child in quintile III would attend a tertiary institution is reasonably high—though still lower—when compared to the same probability for a child in quintile V, but the probability that the institution will be public is much higher in quintile III than in quintile V. Thus, the product of these two probabilities, namely the probability that a child in quintile III or IV will attend a university, *and* that this university will be public, is quite high. Also, of course, the income per family in quintile III is much lower than for in quintile V. These three factors mean that the relative incidence of spending on tertiary education favors quintiles III and IV. Public university subsidies are much more important to the middle class than to the upper-income or lower-income quintiles. This, of course, explains their political popularity.

Correlations Between Spending and Poverty Within the Public Sector

It was noted above that the relatively pro-poor nature of public spending on education is to a large degree a matter of private choice rather than public policy. Public spending on education might not be actively targeted or preferential to the poor. Instead, richer families simply have less children, and opt to send them to private schools because the quality of public schools is seen as mediocre. This section explores the issue of whether spending *within* public education itself favors or disfavors the poor. That is, the section assesses whether spending in public education favors the poorer among those who attend public schools.

It has been noted, using fairly aggregate data, that spending for various levels of education is negatively correlated with measures of poverty in Peru. Table 4.9 shows per stu-

Table 4.9. Per Student Spending and Poverty Levels by Region, 2003			
Region	Primary	Secondary	Poverty headcount
Amazonas	639	993	61%
Ancash	713	1,194	54%
Apurimac	633	821	68%
Arequipa	776	1,081	42%
Ayacucho	695	948	65%
Cajamarca	618	890	73%
Callao	526	880	41%
Cusco	550	697	56%
Huancavelica	622	943	82%
Huánuco	533	779	78%
Ica	682	916	26%
Junín	596	890	51%
La Libertad	568	893	50%
Lambayeque	514	784	49%
Lima	631	947	37%
Loreto	626	872	66%
Madre de Dios	795	1,014	21%
Moquegua	1,178	1,437	39%
Pasco	645	1,065	61%
Piura	548	766	60%
Puno	722	933	57%
San Martín	653	905	29%
Tacna	776	1,324	25%
Tumbes	1,081	1,739	55%
Ucayali	506	846	61%

Sources: Spending: Public Budget National Bureau, Ministry of Economics and Finance, Students: School Census 2003, Ministry of Education, Poverty: ENAHO 2003/2004, Annual Sample.

dent spending on primary and secondary education and the poverty headcount for each regional authority.

In this table, and as shown in Figure 4.5 (for the case of primary education—the results for secondary education are much the same, so primary education can be taken as the case in point), there is a significant negative linear correlation between spending per student and poverty; −0.53 at the primary level, and −0.56 at the secondary level (−0.59 and −0.57 for a log-log correlation). The elasticity of spending with respect to poverty, at the primary level, is −0.41: every percentage increase in poverty is associated with a 0.41 percent decrease in per student spending. However, the regions are very disparate in population or enrollment. Treating regions as units of observation can thus greatly distort the picture, particularly if some regions are outliers. Figure 4.5 suggests that indeed some regions are outliers (specifically Tumbes and Moquegua, as can be seen in Table 4.9), and that without these outliers the correlation, and more importantly (in this case) the slope of the relationship, is not nearly as high. The less-steep line represents the same relationship, but leaves Moquegua and Tumbes out of the estimation of the curve.

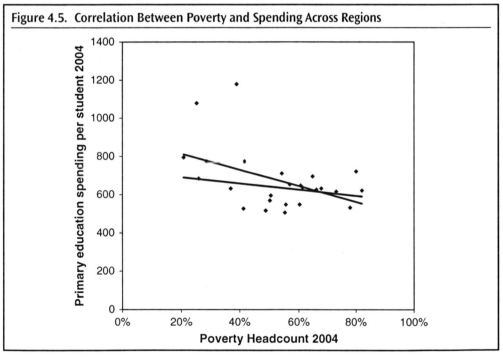

Figure 4.5. Correlation Between Poverty and Spending Across Regions

Source: See Table 4.9.

An analysis that goes down at least to the province level thus seems useful. However, the use of expenditure data can introduce biases. Expenditure tracking in Peru lacks the refinement needed for expenditure to be attributable to the units where the expenditure benefit was received. Many expenditures are allocated or attributed to levels in the system where the purchases or procurements take place but not to the level where the resources are used. This distorts the picture and naturally tends to produce a picture that is more anti-poor than is probably the case, because, for example, the provincial capitals—where purchases are made and the apparent benefits registered—tend to be less poor than the outlying areas. A simple expedient is to analyze not expenditure but instead the pupil-teacher ratio as reported at school level. Another simple expedient is to analyze the correlation between, say, quality of infrastructure and schooling inputs with the socioeconomic level of the parents at schools. Both of these analyses were carried out.

Because teachers are paid very uniformly in Peru, and since teaching costs represent such a large proportion of total education costs, analyzing the distribution of the pupil-teacher ratio by provincial poverty levels is a fairly good proxy for analyzing total expenditure by poverty level. In this analysis, official data on pupils and teachers from the Ministry of Education, and poverty data from FONCODES, were used.[16] This database, then, has both region and province level data. Data at the regional level confirm that for, say, primary education, there is a positive correlation of 0.32 between poverty and the pupil-teacher ratio (hence the poor get less resources), but when the analysis is done at the province level, the linear correlation between poverty and the pupil-teacher ratio is only 0.23. The elasticity is now 0.17: every increase in poverty of 1 percent is associated with a 0.17 percent increase in the pupil-teacher ratio. However, if one controls for the population density of the provinces, the elasticity of the pupil-teacher ratio with respect to poverty increases from 0.17 to 0.25.[17] That is, for areas of equal population density, the poor get a higher pupil-teacher ratio, which translates into a smaller allocation of teachers.

A further analysis was performed using the data from the 2001 National Evaluation (the periodic sample-based learning achievement evaluation).[18] This allows for school-level comparisons, but only on a sample basis. At this level, the relationship between poverty and pupil-teacher ratios disappears, or, in fact, becomes significantly pro-poor. Unfortunately, using school-level data, it is impossible to tell whether this relationship disappears if one controls for population density. It is possible that, if population density and poverty are well correlated (they are somewhat correlated at the provincial level, it is possible that at the school level they would be even more correlated), the lower pupil-teacher ratio observed in poorer schools is due more to low density than to poverty. The fact remains, however, that the distribution of teachers is progressive even within the public sector: the implicit concentration coefficient in the distribution of teachers is *negative* 0.25: the poor do seem to get a disproportionate number of the teachers.

The correlations between the index of socioeconomic status of the parents and the indices of school infrastructure and of supply availability were found to be 0.81 and 0.66 respectively: the richer the parents, the better the infrastructure and supplies. It is not possible to calculate a particularly meaningful elasticity or concentration coefficient for these

---

16. Ministerio de Educación, Unidad de Estadística Educativa, *Cifras de la Educación 1998–2003* using the province-level data, and FONCODES district-wise poverty map with data aggregated up to provincial level.

17. It is important to take density into account because density is an important predictor of the pupil-teacher ratio, and density and poverty are negatively correlated, with a correlation of −0.23. The more densely populated an area, the less poor it tends to be.

18. The analysis was done at the school level, using the variables infra_1, infrau_1, and nse4ps_1, which measure, respectively, the quality of school infrastructure, access to schooling resources, and the parents' socioeconomic status. In addition, the size of the tested class was used as a proxy for the school-level pupil-teacher ratio. The data in the file on mathematics achievement in the 4th grade of primary school were used.

relationships because they are based on indices that take on values below and above 0, and whose absolute value is not clear.[19] Taking a reasonable additive displacement to the indices, the Gini coefficient seems to be somewhere between 0.10 and 0.15. This is much more unequal than the distribution of teachers, but more equal than the distribution of income.

Distribution of Results

The ultimate benefit from education is, of course, not the spending or inputs that are transferred to the poor, but the increase in life chances and labor market options that the poor derive from improved human capital. The latter is unfortunately difficult to evaluate with current data. However, an intermediate proxy is the distribution of learning results. The data on learning results are quite telling. To see this, the 4th grade primary mathematics ("lógico-matemática") in the National Assessment 2001 results were used because essentially all children are in school in the 4th grade. This makes it possible to unambiguously calculate the distribution of results in a manner that parallels calculations related to, say, the distribution of income or total family expenditure. In later grades some children have abandoned the system, which makes it difficult to know what the distribution of results, by income group, might mean; it would tend to overstate the equality of distribution of likely life-chances (to the degree life-chances are determined by schooling results), since only those remaining in school are being evaluated.

There are two important distributional aspects related to the results. First, there is the nature and curvature of the bivariate relationship between results and poverty or social disadvantage. Second, there is the degree to which the distribution of results is comparatively equalizing or not.

The results on the relationship between poverty and learning are shown in Figure 4.6.[20] The variable used to denote learning is the Spanish ("comunicación integral") results, but an analysis using mathematics ("lógico-matemática") shows exactly the same results.

Three points are worth noting. First, the overall relationship is perhaps slightly nonlinear, as can be seen from the shape of the results that are grouped below socioeconomic index level 2 versus the rest of the results in Figure 4.6. Learning in Peru (at least in this key assessment) appears to respond somewhat more steeply to the first improvements in socioeconomic status than to subsequent improvements. To the degree that public expenditure

---

19. It should be noted that while the elasticity and concentration coefficients are ambiguous because the scales of the indices are arbitrary, span 0, and have means close to zero, the correlation coefficient, on the other hand, being invariant to scale, is unambiguous, and there is a clear and high linear correlation between socioeconomic status and public benefits from school infrastructure and access to supplies. The distribution of infrastructure and supplies is poverty-enhancing rather than poverty-fighting.

20. The scale for the vertical axis was set at the minimum and the maximum of the individual student test scores in order to create a better sense of an absolute minimum and maximum. The scaling method used for the learning scores, in the National Assessment 2001, does not have a theoretical minimum or maximum at some unambiguous and simple set of points such as 0 and 100. Setting the minimum at 0 therefore minimizes the range of differences observed in a graphical approach. On the other hand, setting the minimum at the minimum of the school-level results exaggerates the differences because there are few, if any, schools in which *all* students would have performed as badly as theoretically possible. Taking the scores of the worst- and best-performing individual students as the bottom and top ends of the scale seems logical and appropriate for a graphical depiction of the problem.

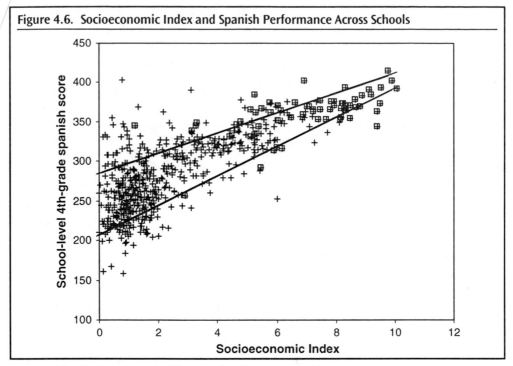

Figure 4.6. Socioeconomic Index and Spanish Performance Across Schools

Source: Calculated and graphed from National Assessment 2001 data.

can be compensatory of private disadvantage (and there is no certainty about this), this result would constitute an efficiency argument for more pro-poor spending. But, second, the relationship for the very poor, while steep, is also more ambiguous and less predictable. This can also be seen in Figure 4.6. Regression lines through the 85th and 15th quantiles are shown to give an idea of how the spread in performance decreases with wealth. That is, at equal levels of poverty among the poor, there is a very large variance in results, whereas among the wealthier there appears to be less variance in results.[21] This suggests that management in schools or areas with poor clients is less effective, either because the school-level management is less responsive and accountable, or because there are, as yet, no models of pedagogical delivery that are effectively reliable for the poor and for those with a linguistic

---

21. This relative compression of the variance of results for the wealthier is unlikely to be due to a bunching up of the results against the top of the scale since, as can be seen, few schools are anywhere close to the top end of the scale—see previous footnote for a discussion of the scale used. That is, in the relevant range the relationship does not appear to be censored from above. Furthermore, beyond the cluster of points represented by the poorest, the reduction in the conditional variance of results seems to take place along the whole socioeconomic spectrum, and from both above and below. There are simply very few schools for the wealthier with very poor results. The nature of this relationship (greater variance in results for the poor) was tested in two ways. First, the absolute value of the error from the bivariate relationship between 4th grade primary Spanish results and the socioeconomic index was regressed on the socioeconomic index, and the result was, as expected, a strongly significant negative relationship ($p < 0.0001$). Second, the interquantile range as a function of the socioeconomic index was also estimated, and this also turns out to be a strong negative relationship. Figure 4.6 shows the lines through the 85th and 15th quantiles respectively. The difference between these two quantiles at the horizontal origin is 78, whereas at the value of 10 on the horizontal axis, the difference is only 21.

disadvantage. (Or else that poor schools are less predictably provided—and not simply less provided—with inputs than wealthier ones. But this is not the case. While the poor do indeed get less input, the variance in input supply to the poor is no greater than the variance in input supply to the less poor. This issue is dealt with below and elsewhere in this report.) The important point to note is that there are sources of inequality of results that are not poverty-related, and yet these sources of inequality seem to operate more powerfully precisely *among* the poor. In other words, it seems as if the poor are more subject than the less-poor to the inequality introduced by loose management, loose accountability, and the unreliability of the pedagogical models used.

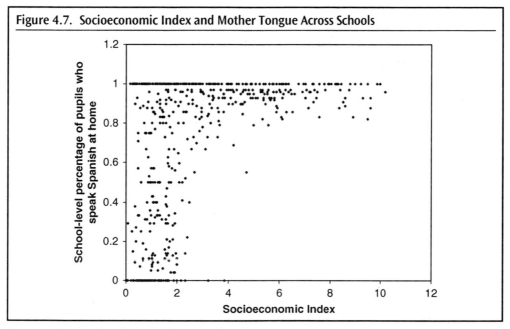

Figure 4.7. Socioeconomic Index and Mother Tongue Across Schools

Source: Calculated and graphed from National Assessment 2001 data.

There are two other sources of variation among the poor that account for some of the variation in results.

First, the language spoken at home. While many of the poor come from a non-Spanish speaking environment, only a few of the better-off come from such environments. This is clearly shown in Figure 4.7. Thus, the larger variability in schooling results among the poor is partly due to larger variability of linguistic origin among the poor. Educational packages for the poor need to be sensitive to linguistic variability. A great deal of attention is paid to this in Chapter 8.

However, a reasonable question is whether the greater variation in home language among the poor is behind the greater variation of results among the poor. To see whether this might be the case, one can take the residuals of a regression of learning results on home language, and then see whether those residuals still show greater variance among the poor than among the rich. The results are shown in Figure 4.8.

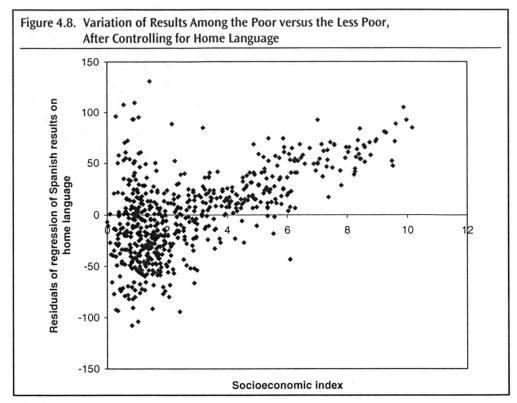

Figure 4.8. Variation of Results Among the Poor versus the Less Poor, After Controlling for Home Language

Source: Calculated and graphed from National Assessment 2001 data.

In fact, if one controls for home language there is still a great deal of variation among the poor. The *relatively* higher variability among the poor than among the less poor is in fact 60 percent greater after controlling for home language. The way to interpret this is as follows. There is greater variability of results among poor people of equally non-Spanish origin than among less-poor people of equally non-Spanish origin. This again suggests that the issue is not just the lack of good pedagogical models for the bilingual or for those whose home language is not Spanish but that—and completely aside from issues of home language—the poor are subject to greater variability of educational standards than the rich in terms of management and capable pedagogy. Luck counts for more in, for example, finding a good and responsible teacher, if one is poor than if one is rich. The poor have not only worse teachers, but they have teachers whose behavior or quality is also much less consistent (including less consistently bad).

Second, there is the issue of nutrition. Not all of the poor are equally malnourished. While the poor are typically less well nourished than the non-poor, there is greater nourishment variability among the poor than among the non-poor, as Figure 4.9 shows. Poverty is hardly a good indicator of nutritional need. In fact, the top of the nourishment distribution is essentially flat, and the relationship between socioeconomic status and nutrition is somewhat like a right triangle, in which many of the poor are as well-nourished as the well-off but few of the well-off are malnourished. Note that, unfortunately, no strong database could be found with both nutritional or anthropometric data and learning results data on the same children. Thus, the direct impact of nutrition on learning could not be established, and there is not much in the Peruvian literature on this issue. Nonetheless, the results are telling. Improving the educational results among the poor, and picking up the lower end of the distribution, likely means being able to improve nutrition as well as educational standards. However, by the time children reach school most of the nutritional damage is done. Thus, unless some creative way is found to use schools to reach the poor before they are even in school, ensuring as such that the nutrition of future young scholars can be improved via the education system, the problem is likely to remain more intersectoral than educational. In any case, to propose that teachers should be made responsible for the nutritional status of children in the 0–5 age range in their villages would require considerable further analysis.

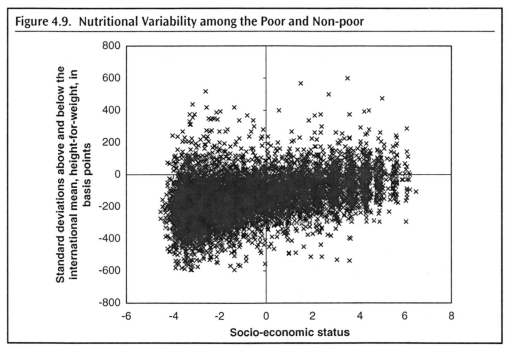

Figure 4.9. Nutritional Variability among the Poor and Non-poor

Source: Calculated from the *Encuesta Demográfica y de Salud Familiar* (ENDES) 2000. The indicator used was height-for-age in terms of standard deviations from the international benchmark mean, as expressed as basis points.

Unfortunately, it was impossible to see whether the observed phenomenon of greater learning variation among the poor remains once one takes into account the greater nutritional variation for the same group because the large student achievement databases do not include data on nutritional status. As should be noted from the analysis just carried out on language, the mere fact that there is greater variability in nutritional status among the poor (just as there is greater variability in home language among the poor) cannot be taken as indicative that if one corrects for nutrition, the greater variability in learning results among the poor will disappear.

A third point to note is that the results of public and private schools seem about equally sensitive to poverty, including the problem of greater heterogeneity of results among the poor. This last point is merely suggestive, as there are not enough data points for private schools to make this a safe conclusion. Figure 4.6, above, shows private schools with a square symbol imposed on the symbol for all schools. This demonstrates essentially the same patterns of relationship between socioeconomic status and achievement for private schools as for public schools.

It is unlikely that the variance of results among the poor is simply due to a variance of input provision among the same group since the variance of results as driven by input provision is itself also greater at low levels of input provision, and since the variance in input supply to the poorer is not higher—if anything it is lower—than variance in input supply to the less poor. Figure 4.10 shows greater variance in learning at low levels of input provision than at higher levels of input provision: the same pattern seen in response to socioeconomic status. This is shown both for infrastructure and general supplies in the same figure.

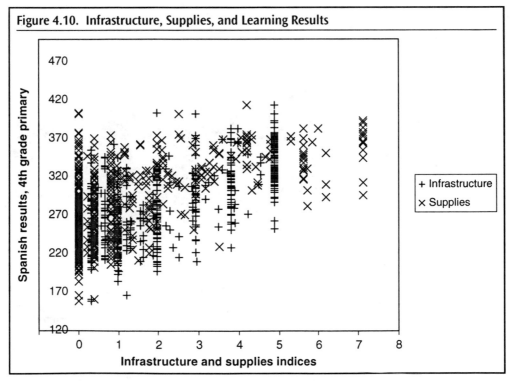

Figure 4.10. Infrastructure, Supplies, and Learning Results

Source: Calculated and graphed from National Assessment 2001 data.

Figure 4.11 and Figure 4.12 make the point that input supply to the poor appears to be no more variable than input supply to the rich—on the contrary, while the poor are worse-supplied than the rich, they are more predictably badly supplied than the rich are well-supplied. As shown by the quantile regression lines in Figure 4.11 and Figure 4.12, there is actually *less* variability among the poor in the supply of, say, infrastructure, precisely because they are the recipients of uniformly bad infrastructure.[22] Thus, greater *variability* of results among the poor seems unlikely to be caused mainly by greater *variability* in input supply to the poor, even if poorer results among the poor are partly caused by less input supply. As has been seen, variance in results among the poor is very large. Instead, the explanation seems to be that the poor receive the worst management and are subjected to untested as well as inappropriate pedagogical methods (for their culture and needs), which produce highly variable results instead of simply uniformly bad results amongst the group in question.

The second aspect of the relationship between poverty and results is the distribution of results by income group, or the concentration coefficient of the results. For this result, we used data from the results of the National Assessment 2001 for 4th grade Spanish ("comunicación integral"). To calculate the concentration coefficient of results distribution across

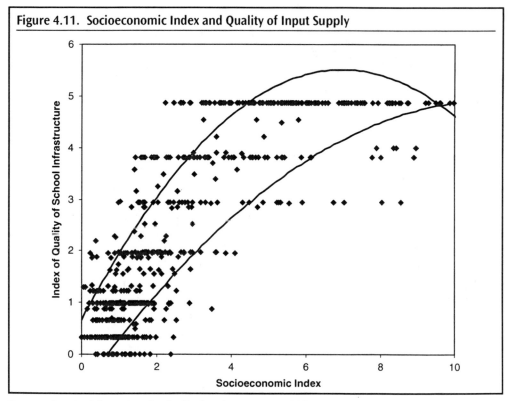

Figure 4.11. Socioeconomic Index and Quality of Input Supply

Source: Graphed from data in the National Assessment 2001.

---

22. The quantile regressions are non-linear (quadratic) in Figure 4.11 to capture the fact that the general relationship, and its conditional variance, seem to be non-linear. The regressions are through the 85th and 15th quantiles (25th in Figure 4.12). Whether the variance ultimately begins to decrease toward the very top of the income distribution (after widening for the less-poor in general) is difficult to say and probably not very important. This analysis is carried out with all schools (public and private). An analysis was also carried out with only public schools and the basic results are not different.

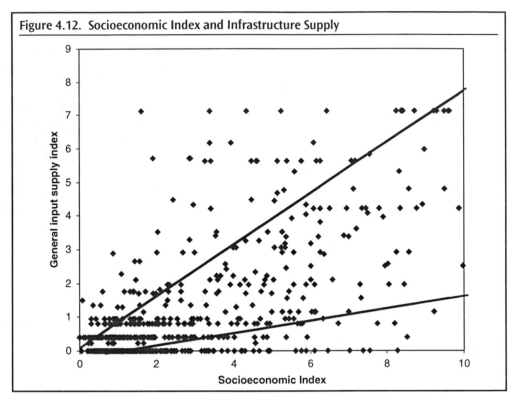

Figure 4.12. Socioeconomic Index and Infrastructure Supply

Source: Graphed from data in the National Assessment 2001.

schools, they were ranked according to the socioeconomic index of the families of the children in the schools. To make the results comparable to the concept of "income," the lowest value in the results was reset to zero, and all the other values were reset by subtracting the lowest value. The resulting concentration coefficient was 0.12. It should be noted that this is not the "pure" inequality of the results themselves (that is, the results were not used to rank the students—socioeconomic status was). Instead, this is the concentration coefficient of the results incidence by socioeconomic group. It is also to be noted that the ranking criterion was the socioeconomic status as provided by the National Assessment. In any case, the result is that learning achievement in Peru is distributed somewhat unequally but much more equally than income or private expenditure on education.

This section has shown that poverty is strongly predictive of learning results, but that this relationship weakens considerably *among* the poor. It has also argued that the distribution of results should matter more—as a social goal—than the distribution of inputs. It has shown that the distribution of the most expensive input, namely teachers, seems to favor the poor if the analysis is done at a sufficiently micro level (though most likely, judging from the evidence at the province level, this is not so much because they are poor but because those who are poorest happen to live in areas that are sparsely populated, and hence it is difficult to achieve a high pupil-teacher ratio). In this respect, it is logical to be concerned with whether the distribution of teachers at least helps to achieve results. Since teachers represent such a high proportion of total costs, if the pupil-teacher ratio is not predictive of learning results, then, in general, resources are not likely to explain results. Along these lines, tracking the pupil-teacher ratio as a matter of cost would make sense but not because it is an important correlate of quality.

Figure 4.13 and Figure 4.14 show the correlation between results and the pupil-teacher ratio, using 4th grade primary Spanish results as a case in point. The first figure shows the relationship between the pupil-teacher ratio and the actual results. It shows essentially no relationship (or indeed

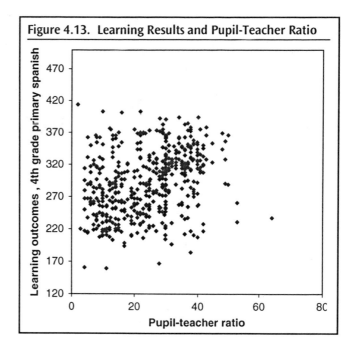

Figure 4.13. Learning Results and Pupil-Teacher Ratio

a counter-intuitive relationship: the higher the pupil-teacher ratio, the better the results) between the pupil-teacher ratio and the results (r = 0.32). However, this may be due to the influence of other factors. As noted, lower pupil-teacher ratios are associated with poverty (probably because poverty is associated with low population density). If lower pupil-teacher ratios exert a positive influence on results holding poverty constant, but poverty exerts a negative influence, then the impact of the pupil-teacher ratio, if one does not hold poverty constant, would be very weak or actually positive (if poverty exerts a very strong influence, and the poor have much lower pupil-teacher ratios). To assess this, the second figure shows the impact of the pupil-teacher ratio on the residuals of a regression that controls for all other likely factors.[23] This shows no relationship (r = −0.01). This lack of relationship is a particular concern in light of the result, discussed elsewhere in this report, showing that teacher expenditure is crowding out most other forms of expenditure in the sector. In sum, it appears as if a great deal of cost goes towards an input that shows little correlation with learning results.

We thus have a situation where poverty is generally predictive of results, and where results are therefore regressively distributed. Furthermore, we have observed large variations in results among the poor for factors that have little to do with poverty itself. We have shown that there is little relationship between the key input, the pupil-teacher ratio, and results. Thus, it seems a safe conclusion that the variability in results among the poor is more related to management—in a broad sense (accountability, existence of effective and reliable instructional models and standards, etc.)—than to anything else.

---

23. The model used was a school (or, in fact, classroom) level model using poverty, children's mother tongue, whether the region is bilingual, private vs. public ownership of the school, whether the children work during the week, and how well the teachers prepare for class. This model has considerable explanatory power ($R^2 = 0.73$).

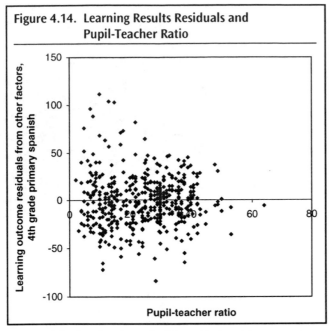

Figure 4.14.   Learning Results Residuals and Pupil-Teacher Ratio

Source: Calculated and graphed from National Assessment 2001 data.

Summary of Inequality of Benefits

The following table summarizes various concepts of distribution of benefits, focusing on primary education as an important case in point.

Education spending looks most pro-poor if one considers the distribution of students attending public education across income quintiles, which implicitly assumes equal spending per student (row 1). If one relaxes this assumption and allows for unequal spending per student in public education, then spending seems

Table 4.10.   Summary on Inequality of Various Educational Benefits

Concept	Concentration coefficient
1. Distribution of beneficiaries attending public schools, in primary education, across all income quintiles (assumes equal per student spending across quintiles.)	−0.28
2. Distribution of public spending ("benefits") on public schools in primary education across all income quintiles (allows spending to vary by quintile.)	−0.26
3. Distribution of pupil-teacher ratio within public primary schools.	−0.26
4. Distribution of pupil-teacher ratio (including public and private primary schools).	−0.14
5. Distribution of infrastructure and supplies to beneficiaries within primary public education.	0.10–0.15 or as high as 0.34 for specific inputs, such as electricity in public schools.
6. Distribution of learning results in Spanish, 4th grade primary, across all (public and private) schools.	0.12
7. Total private spending on education (private spending in public and private schools on uniforms, books, PTA fees, instructional fees, etc.).	0.55
8. Distribution of total household expenditure.	0.45–0.50

Source: Calculated by the authors as explained in the text.

a little less pro-poor (row 2). The distribution of teachers in the sector as a whole (hence teachers paid for with public and private funds, in public and private schools) is progressive (row 4), but less so than the distribution of public benefits. The distribution of teachers within the public sector is about the same as the distribution of expenditure across income quintiles (row 3). The distribution of infrastructural and supply inputs is anti-poor (row 5). The distribution of learning results in the society (row 6, taking both public and private schools) is much more unequal than the distribution of resources under any definition (except perhaps for infrastructure resources). The distribution of private spending on education is the most unequal distribution (row 7) in the table. This distribution might go a long way towards explaining why the distribution of results is more unequal than the distribution of public resources: private expenditure on education is considerable, and very unequally distributed (in fact, more unequal than total private expenditure). The distribution of results is much more equal than the distribution of total private family expenditure (rows 8 and 6), which mirrors the distribution of income (the distribution of income is probably somewhat more unequal than the distribution of expenditure, but income data in the household surveys used in this study are not as reliable as expenditure data). In this sense, and in spite of the productivity and distribution problems in the sector, it should be noted that the sector's results are still equalizing (to the degree that learning results may be somewhat predictive of future income). However, given the large variance in results among the poor, it is also clear that the situation could be improved—education could in principle be made somewhat more equalizing. It is true that better distribution of resources is a constraint to better results, in principle, because (to the degree publicly-provided resources can compensate for poverty) results improve with reductions in poverty. Yet, if one attempted to use fiscal or resource transfers as a sort of "income replacement" (given the association between poverty and results), it should be noted that particularly among the poor, the response of results to socioeconomic status is unpredictable: the variance of results among the poor, for any given level of socioeconomic status, is higher than for higher levels of socioeconomic status. This suggests that the sequencing of reform should be to improve management (understood broadly to include not only more accountability for results and standards, but also the development and spread of pedagogical and other support models that are *predictably* effective at improving learning among the poor) of schools, particularly where the poor are the clients, and then increase spending among the poor in ways that can (partially) compensate for their poverty either through redistribution or through improved overall spending.

As a methodological conclusion, finally, the gap between the −0.28 in the first row, and the 0.12 in the sixth row is notable and suggests that standard incidence analysis could be quite misleading, if what one cares about is learning. Primary education provision, writ large (looking across the public and private sectors) and considering learning itself, is much less equalizing than traditional "benefit" analysis (where "benefit" is taken to be proxied by spending) would normally lead one to believe.

Special Focus on Teacher Costs

Labor costs in Peruvian education are generally recognized as crowding out other inputs. This is covered in previous sections of this report, where it is shown just how quickly salary costs are increasing as a share of total expenditure. This section assesses the sources of this pressure, and whether the pressure is in some sense justified with respect to some benchmarks. Two sources of pressure are considered: the pupil-teacher ratio, which drives the total number of teachers (assuming enrollment growth is low, which, as has been noted previously, is the case) and the cost per teacher. This section also assesses to what degree there has been some protection for some other key inputs, specifically textbooks.

Pupil-teacher Ratio Decrease as a Source of Pressure

Table 4.11 shows the basic data on the pupil-teacher ratio in Peru and in the rest of Latin America. A few factors stand out. First, in terms of the average level and the rate of change, Peru is close to the median for Latin America—though lower for secondary education. Almost all countries tend to lower their pupil-teacher ratios over time as they grow economically (and partly as a result of social pressures and expectations, not only because a lower ratio becomes more affordable with growth). Peru and Latin America in general are no exception, and Peru is not outside the norm for Latin America. However, if one considers the fact that Peru's GDP per capita is considerably lower than that for Latin America as a whole (which would suggest a higher pupil-teacher ratio), then Peru's pupil-teacher ratios seem a little lower than is justified.[24] Using a GDP-driven norm, Peru's expected pupil-teacher ratio, at the primary level, would be about 26.4 in the year 2000 and 20.6 at the secondary level.[25] This is a little higher than the actual values in 2000 for primary and considerably higher than the actual value for secondary, though some of this could be due to measurement or reporting errors. (Ratios tend to be over-reported in international data, whereas Peru's ratios (below) are from the country's own sources.) It seems a safe conclusion that the pressure on non-salary expenditure does come partially from too low a pupil-teacher ratio. This is particularly the case if one considers that lowering the pupil-teacher ratio is by no means a necessary condition for education success, as much research and the experience of East Asia in the 1970s and 1980s demonstrates (though population densities there are much higher than in Latin America, which makes high pupil-teacher ratios administratively feasible). Note that none of Peru's own research, as reported in Chapter 2, suggests that lowering the pupil-teacher ratio has a positive impact on learning, much less a cost-effective impact. And it is particularly striking when one notes, as is made clear elsewhere in this report, that low pupil-teacher ratios are at not at all correlated with greater achievement in Peruvian education.

However, in explaining the current dynamics of pressure on the budget, the rate of change in the pupil-teacher ratio, rather than its level compared to the rest of Latin America, is the most important issue. Table 4.11 shows that this ratio has been decreasing over the past few years at a rate fairly consistent with that of the rest of Latin America, in spite of the fact that the ratio is already fairly low in Peru.

---

24. The Latin America-wide correlation between the primary pupil-teacher ratio and (the logarithm of) GDP per capita is 0.6. At the secondary level it is 0.42.

25. It might be argued that an important determinant of the pupil-teacher ratio is population density, and that, because Peru has a lower population density than other Latin American countries, it is reasonable to expect a lower pupil-teacher ratio. However, the Latin America-wide correlation between the pupil-teacher ratio and population density is only −0.12. In any case, if one includes population density in an equation to drive an expectation of pupil-teacher ratios, the expected value for Peru does not change. The expected value is still a little higher than the actual value: Peru's pupil-teacher ratios are thus a little lower than expected.

Table 4.11. Pupil Teacher Ratios in Peru and Average for Latin America							
	1998	1999	2000	2001	2002	2003	LA MRE
Primary urban	24.5	24.3	23.6	23.5	23.1	22.4	NA
Secondary urban	17.7	17.9	17.3	17.3	17.4	16.8	NA
Primary rural	26.9	27.0	26.3	25.9	24.9	24.4	NA
Secondary rural	14.0	14.3	14.4	14.8	14.8	15.0	NA
Primary total	25.4	25.3	24.6	24.4	23.7	23.1	23.9
Secondary total	17.1	17.2	16.8	16.8	16.9	16.4	19.2
Yearly decrease, primary, average 1998–2003				−1.9%			−1.8%
Yearly decrease, secondary				−0.7%			NA
Yearly decrease, total				−1.7%			NA

Sources:
Peruvian data: *Ministerio de Educación, Unidad de Estadística Educativa, Cifras de la Educación 1998–2003.* Latin America data: EDSTATS.
Note:
Secondary pupil-teacher data for Latin America as a whole are available for too short a period to permit estimation of a trend.

The sources of pressures on teacher numbers can be summarized as follows: student numbers (in primary and secondary—the bulk of the students) have been growing at 0.9 percent, and the number of teachers has been growing at 2.6 percent. The resultant pupil-teacher ratio has therefore been growing at −1.7 percent. As a source of pressure on the numbers of teachers, then, growth in enrollment is one-third of the pressure, and growth in the pupil-teacher ratio is two-thirds of the pressure.

Recent Salary Increases as a Source of Pressure

The second overall source of pressure on costs is teacher salaries. Table 4.12 shows the evolution of teacher salaries over the last few years.

Table 4.12. Teacher Salaries in Peru, 1999–2004			
Year	Total monthly Pay	Increase	Date of increase
1999 (year-start)	730.33	108.26	April 1999
2000 (year-start)	838.59	None	NA
2001	838.59	None	NA
2002	838.59	None	NA
2003 (year-end)	938.59	100	May 2003
2004 (year-end)	1053.59	70, then 45	May, August 2003
Percent increase 2004/1999 (year-start)		7.6%	
Percent increase 2004/1999 (year-end)		4.7%	

Note: Uses level III teacher working 30 hours as a case in point.
Source: Ministry of Education, *Secretaría de Planificación Estratégica.*

Because the increases often take place sometime after the start of the year (in 2004 they took place in May and August), it is difficult to know when to calculate a year-on-year percentage increase. Taking both of the calculations reported in Table 4.12 (7.6 percent and 4.7 percent), we get an average of 6.1 percent. In a previous section we noted that, calculating on the basis of whole fiscal years, the growth in the labor bill has been 8.6 percent. This can now be de-composed into approximately 6.1 percent for salary increases, and 2.6 percent for increases in numbers of teachers.

Taking all of these pressures into account, the total pressure on the salary bill can be decomposed (in round numbers) as follows:

- 70 percent due to salary increases
- 30 percent due to increases in teacher numbers, of which
  - 20 percent is due to improvements (decreases) in the pupil-teacher ratio
  - 10 percent is due to the growth in enrollments.

It seems fairly clear that further reductions in the pupil-teacher ratio should be carefully resisted. Note, however, that this has been only 20 percent of the pressure on total salary costs. Further increases in salaries need to be justified by way of a more thorough assessment of whether salaries are too low relative to various norms. In any case, increases should be tied to accountability measures.

Is the Absolute Level of Teacher Salaries Low in Peru?

Whether the pressure from increases in teacher salaries is justified in Peru is related to whether salaries are low, or have been low in the recent past. Evidently, if salaries are "too low," then some upward pressure, for some time, is justified. Unfortunately the evidence on this issue, for Peru as well as for the rest of Latin America, is not very good.

A relatively simple strategy is to compare teacher salaries, or total teacher compensation, to GDP per capita. The OECD has carried out such comparisons (OECD 2005). In Peru, teachers at the top of the salary scale earn the same as GDP per capita: the ratio of teacher salaries to GDP per capita is 1.0. In Latin America as a whole, this ratio is 1.35. However, this refers to a 20-hour teaching load and most teachers in Peru work more than this, so the comparison is not satisfying.

It has become common in Peru to decry the fact that teachers some decades ago earned much better salaries (the peak was 1966—see Díaz and Saavedra 2000); they were considered to be of a higher social class than is the case today. It is clear that relative salaries have dropped in Peru when compared with previous decades. Yet, this phenomenon is actually fairly typical of development. In very poor African countries, the ratio of teacher earnings to GDP per capita is often as high as 5.0 or even more. In poor countries, teachers are an elite. As development proceeds, teachers tend to originate, more and more, from the middle of the social spectrum. The same OECD data show that in developing countries as a whole, teacher salaries as a ratio of GDP per capita are at 1.96, whereas for developed countries they are at 1.33. Data compiled by Carnoy and Welmond (no date) show a clear negative relationship between GDP per capita and the ratio of teacher costs to GDP per capita (t-value = 7.8). This relationship is non-linear: as countries move from low-income to middle-income status, teacher salaries relative to GDP per capita drop extremely quickly, and then drop much less steeply (or barely at all) as countries move to high-income status. It stands to reason that when skills related to literacy, such as those possessed by teachers, are very scarce (as in the poorest countries), the cost of acquiring those skills for the education sector is high. As a consequence, when teachers are expensive, only a minority of the population can be educated if the total education budget is to remain affordable to the taxpayers. Peru has created a mass education system which has been affordable through relatively low pay for teachers—a process that is typical of development. However, it may be that teachers in Peru are more poorly compensated than is explainable by this general historical tendency common to most societies. And, it is undeniable that real pay for teachers in Peru has dropped enormously in the last few decades.

The most detailed studies, such as Hernani Limarino's recent paper (2004), use quantitative techniques to compare the pay of teachers and non-teachers in Latin America in such a way as to "control" for various factors. For example, teachers generally do earn more than other citizens, but they are also more educated. When one compares teachers to non-teachers "controlling" for the level of education, some of the pay advantage in favor of teachers disappears, yet some remains. Hernani Limarino (2004) concludes that Peruvian teachers, even in 2000, were actually a little better paid than the relevant comparison groups—and salaries have gone up since then. Furthermore, teachers might work fewer hours over the year; so if one controls for hours worked, the pay advantage appears even stronger. However, all these studies are unable to control for the most important factor: the *quality* of education received by teachers, and the inherent skill of teachers as compared to other persons with similar years of education. Typically it is not the most talented in many societies that choose teaching as a profession, especially as development proceeds; this is the case in Peru. Thus, 14 or 15 years of education for a teacher is not the same thing as 14 or 15 years of education for, say, an engineer. The studies in question also fail to control for complex issues related to the role of teaching in the household's income strategy. In this respect, these studies are ultimately not very satisfying.

The simple fact is that, even at the salaries that have been common in Peru in the last few years, there has been an over-supply of teachers (Díaz and Saavedra 2000). The system annually produces some three times as many teachers as are needed, and there is a great stock of unemployed teachers. This clearly means that teaching at current salaries and even at the lower salaries common a few years ago is attractive for certain segments of the population. The real question is whether these are the segments of the population that society really desires as teachers, and this is not answered by the existing studies. It is possible that the majority of newer Peruvian teachers and potential teachers, who are so attracted to teaching that they cause an over-supply, and who might have relatively poor education themselves, have only informal sector employment as an alternative to teaching. Furthermore, as Webb and Valencia (2006) have argued, a low-effort, low-pay (relative to the past) situation has turned into a "low-level" equilibrium. Teaching (particularly in a public school) is now seen by teachers as a low-effort, low-pay, but high-certainly element in a long-run income portfolio that includes other occupations or teaching in private schools in addition to the "default" low-effort job in a public school. This equilibrium is hard to upset, as all actors have re-structured their lives around it. Simply increasing pay will not break this equilibrium, as the experience of the last few years has shown. Increasing salaries, might, over time, begin to attract a better quality of entrant into the profession, but this would take a very long time indeed to affect the quality of the stock, as the flow rate into the profession is extremely low and would tend to become even lower with across-the-board salary increases. Thus, improved salaries are a worthwhile policy option only if the system is able to administratively distinguish and keep good as opposed to poor candidates via selection by testing, rewards linked to real skill and performance, and other means. There is no point in generating a nominal over-supply if this oversupply cannot be used to drive up the quality of actual entrants into the profession as well as that of those who remain in it. Yet the teacher unions, and to some degree the political classes, have often been resistant to such selection measures (even though individual teachers may favor selection and merit-pay measures—see Rivero 2002). Furthermore, as noted above, salaries have increased in recent times. For all these reasons further salary increases should be resisted until better selection and career progression methods are devised and firmly implanted—methods that do in fact select individuals with more skill and devotion to enter and stay in the profession.

Other Input Supplies

In a previous section it was noted that salaries as a proportion of total expenditure have increased from 71 percent of total expenditure in 1999 to 75 percent in 2005. This is a significant change. The biggest compensatory change, making room for the increase in salaries as a proportion of spending, has been a significant decline in investment and in other capital expenditures. Financial investment, debt amortization, and interest repayment have in any case been a small part of capital expenditure, and have not, as a proportion, changed much. As can be seen in the previous section, expenditure on goods and services has generally not suffered—it has been maintained at about 12 or 13 percent of total expenditure. More specifically, provision of items such as textbooks has been protected, and, as Table 4.13 shows, provision has been maintained.

Unlike teachers, whose cost takes up so much of the budget and shows little or no relationship to learning, the provision or access to other materials does show some relationship to measured learning. As noted in many other sections, the relationship is weakest with low levels of provision: there tend to be fewer materials in poor areas, and in those areas the provision of materials is less predictably associated with learning results. Figure 4.15 and Figure 4.16 make these two points: first, poorer schools do have less supplies—and supplies do make a difference (they make a difference in a multivariate context as well)—but they make a less predictable difference among the poor, which means that supplies can and should be maintained, and if possible, should be more focused on the poor; second, management, particularly in schools in poor areas, needs to be tightened up so as to increase the predictability with which supplies lead to improved performance.[26] Nonetheless, while management can be improved, it is important to insist on continuing to provide these sorts of inputs since they are among the few that seem to have a fairly clear relationship to learning.

---

26. Both figures use the data from the 2001 National Assessment, namely the socioeconomic index of students, the index of supplies or inputs at school (other than infrastructure) and the results in 4th grade primary Spanish. The correlation was established with the overall index of educational resources, not with books as such. Note also that there is no distinction made here between publicly-provided inputs and those obtained by a school with its own resources.

Table 4.13. Textbook Provision in Peru: Selected Data

	Purchased, per child in primary school	Availability at UGEL level	Availability per child
1999	1.65		0.83
2000	1.79		0.90
2001	2.23		1.11
2002	2.10		1.05
2003	1.75	1.76	0.88
2004		2.23	1.11

Notes:
Column 1 is the number of textbooks in Spanish ("Comunicación Integral") and Mathematics ("Lógico-Matemática") purchased by the Ministry, divided by the total number of students enrolled.
Column 2 is the number of textbooks per child in the same two subjects at UGEL level
Column 3 is the result of dividing column 1 or 2 by 2, since in principle children are to receive two texts.
Sources:
Column 1: *Consejo Nacional de Educación,* MAPEI Information Database
Column 2: From Presentation by JP Silva, October 5, 2004, "Sistema de Seguimiento del Gasto Público" at Workshop on Protected Social Programs, Lima, Perú, October 5, 2004.
Column 3: From Presentation by JP Silva, October 5, 2004, "Sistema de Seguimiento del Gasto Público" at Workshop on Protected Social Programs, Lima, Perú, October 5, 2004.

Figure 4.15. Socioeconomic Index and School Supplies

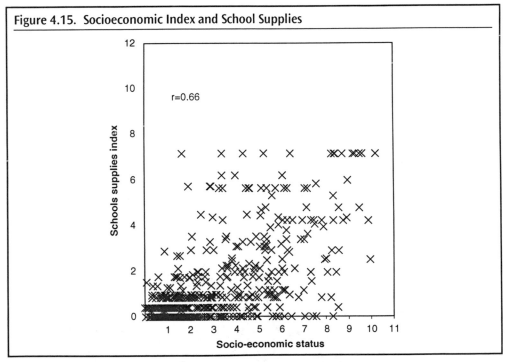

Source: Calculated and graphed from National Assessment 2001 data.

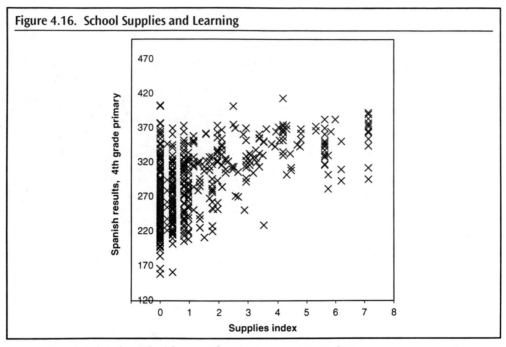

Figure 4.16. School Supplies and Learning

Source: Calculated and graphed from National Assessment 2001 data.

CHAPTER 5

Why Don't Some Peruvian Children Finish High School?[27]

It has been noted that about 65 percent of Peruvian children finish high school. Hence, the cumulative dropout rate is about 35 percent. Whether this can be considered a problem is a matter of perspective. By Latin American standards, this cumulative dropout rate is fairly low—that is, Peru has a high secondary school completion rate. Not only that, but using a world-wide perspective (i.e., comparing to countries such as Korea or Thailand), Peru is much further behind on learning achievement at the secondary level than it is on high-school completion. This was also demonstrated above. Peru's education system is heavily unbalanced toward access and completion in comparison to that of other countries, and biased against actual learning. Nonetheless, policy authorities may wish to address the dropout issue. In that case, it is important to ascertain why youths drop out. The main policy conclusion of this Chapter is that, at least at the current margin, the accessibility of secondary schools does not appear to be the problem. Hence, building schools, as a main policy action, is not a recommended means to address the dropout problem. Most likely, demand stimulation measures, such as conditional cash transfers, would be needed. This is not to say schools are currently under-utilized or that the pattern of distribution of infrastructure of acceptable quality is equitable. It may be that school building in the past has actually been fairly well reactive, in an endogenous sense, to existing local demand. In this case, schools could be more or less well utilized and yet not be a constraint to further enrollment, meaning there is an equilibrium. Furthermore,

---

27. This section is based on the author's interpretation of "Análisis de la deserción escolar en el Perú: evidencias a partir de encuestas y de técnicas cualitativas," by Lorena Alcázar and Néstor Valdivia of GRADE. The work of Pablo Lavado on estimating rates of return to education was also particularly valuable in this section.

it is clear that the quality of infrastructure for the poor is worse than for the better off, as described above. Both of these facts suggest that while one should not be cavalier about infrastructure in general, quantity of infrastructure does not seem to be the main constraint to further enrollment, or greater retention. This section documents the reasons that do seem to be associated with dropping out behavior in Peru.

The Quantitative Evidence

The numerical evidence, based on surveys, is clear. Table 5.1, which uses two independent surveys, makes it clear that the distance to school—or lack of school availability—as a factor contributing to drop-out behavior is a distant fourth reason (among a set of four main reasons) and does not amount to more than about 5 percent of the dropouts, even in rural areas. Economic reasons in general are far and away the most important reason for dropping out. Among women specifically, and taking a broader age group, family reasons are about as important as economic reasons. There are some differences between urban and rural areas—in urban areas dropouts are more likely to find work, or to state that they dropped out in order to work. In rural areas school non-availability is a more important factor, but the problem still does not amount to more than 5 percent of the dropouts. To put things in perspective, out of a typical cohort of, say, 16 or 17 year-olds, around 35 percent are not finishing high school, and of these about 3 percent claim to have dropped out because there is no school nearby. Thus, having no nearby school is a problem that seems to affect only some 1 percent of any given cohort of youths. In the rural areas the problem is worse. 70 percent of children do not finish high school. Yet even here, only 5 percent claim to drop out due to lack of schooling facilities, suggesting that lack of schooling infrastructure affects only some 3.5 percent of rural youths.

If one assumes that "economic reasons" refer to a combination of inability to pay school fees, availability of work or need to work, as well as other factors related to poverty such as the need to help around the house, it seems that poverty is, generically, the key determinant of dropping out behavior. The policy implication appears straightforward: either generic poverty-fighting, or some form of conditional cash-transfer mechanism would be needed to deal with the dropout problem.

Other reasons are important. Family and health issues (including pregnancy) are the second most important cause of dropping out, particularly among females. School quality and relevance, as the third most important factor, are responsible for a large proportion of dropping out behavior.

Aside from direct questions regarding reasons for dropping out, it is possible to indirectly ascertain the correlates of dropping out behavior. The following three graphs, using data from the 2004 ENAHO, show three possible correlates of dropping out behavior: income or socioeconomic status, place of residence, and gender, in that order. The ratio of enrolled population to total population, by age, is taken as an index of dropout behavior. The graphs make it very clear that income and place of residence are important correlates of dropping out behavior, whereas gender is not.

It is also possible to look at similar data by grade, rather than age. One can take enrollment in any grade minus repetition in that grade (if available), divided by the population

Table 5.1. Quantitative Evidence on School Dropping Out

Explicit reasons for dropping out, as provided by dropouts (respondents aged 6–25 who where not in school and had not finished secondary school)

	Rural	Urban	Total
1. Military service	0.5	0.5	0.5
2. Working	10.6	24.9	16.1
3. No adult learning center nearby	0.6	0.3	0.5
4. No school nearby	4.4	0.2	2.8
5. Not interested or don't like school	12.5	12.3	12.4
6. Illness	3.7	5.7	4.5
7. Economic problems	37.1	33.4	35.7
8. Family problems	18.2	9.9	15.1
9. Low grades or school failure	1	0.9	1
10. House work	9.6	9.1	9.5
11. Others	1.9	2.6	2.2

Summary reasons	Rural	Urban	Total
Economic (2, 7, 10)	57.3	67.4	61.3
School quality/ appropriateness/ interest (5, 9)	13.5	13.2	13.4
Family problems and health (6, 8)	21.9	15.6	19.6
No schooling facilities (3, 4)	5	0.5	3.3

Reasons for dropping out, women 15–49 not in school

	Rural	Urban	Total
1. Pregnant	10.1	13.8	12
2. Got married	7.4	5.3	8
3. Needed to take care of children	4.7	3.7	4
4. Family needed help	19.2	2.9	3
5. Could not afford school fees	15.8	20.4	20
6. Illness	2.4	2.0	
7. Needed to earn money	9.7	26.1	17
8. Graduated/felt sufficiently educated	2.6	8.3	6
9. Failed entrance exams	0.9	2.2	2
10. Did not like school	14.2	6.1	10
11. School or teachers unavailable	6.1	0.7	2
12. Other or NA	6.8	8.6	11

Summary reasons	Rural	Urban	Total
Economic (5, 7)	25.5	46.5	37.0
School quality/ relevance (8, 9, 10)	17.7	16.7	18.0
Pregnancy and other family reasons (1, 2, 3, 4)	41.5	25.7	27.0
No schooling nearby (10)	6.1	0.7	2.0

Source: ENAHO 2003 (National Household Survey).

Source: ENDES 2000 (Demographic and Family Health Survey).

of the nominally-appropriate age, as an index of dropping out behavior. Unfortunately, ENAHO data on enrollment by grade do not seem very trustworthy (there are odd and difficult-to-explain discontinuities in the data), and do not indicate whether the student is a repeater or not. Instead, Ministry of Education data are used. A small disadvantage with these data is that the denominator of the index is from a projected source (demographic projections from INEI) that is different from the source of the numerator (Ministry of Education management information systems). Nonetheless, the data are useful and confirm

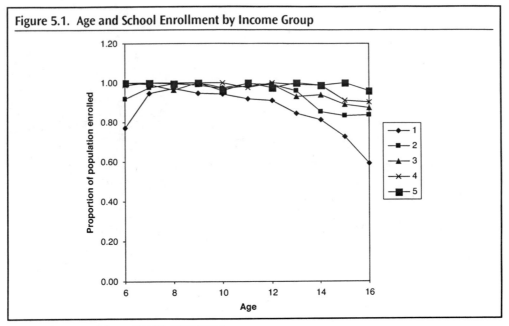

Source: Computed from ENAHO 2003/2004.

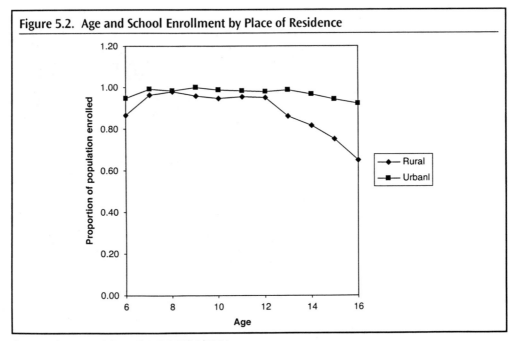

Source: Computed from ENAHO 2003/2004.

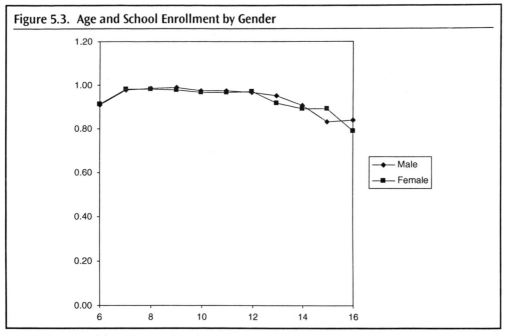

Figure 5.3. Age and School Enrollment by Gender

Source: Computed from ENAHO 2003/2004.

the ENAHO age-based patterns shown above. The following three graphics show the data by place of residence (without correcting for repetition because repetition by place of residence is not easily available) for the country as a whole (with and without repetition correction) and by gender (with repetition correction). Aside from the fact that the data confirm that place of residence (and presumably income) is a much more important correlate of dropping out than gender, the graphs incidentally also show the great importance of repetition in inflating enrollment figures, particularly in the early grades, and specifically in the rural areas. While there is a sudden dropoff in the enrollment patterns between grades 6 and 7 (last of primary and first of secondary), it is interesting that even after controlling for repetition there is a tendency for enrollment in rural areas to drop off continuously throughout the grade career, rather than showing a truly large dropoff between the end of primary and the beginning of secondary. This, together with the fact that repetition is so high, strongly suggests a quality problem that results in an over-age phenomenon as an important co-determinant of eventual dropping out. This then creates a demand side problem as an explanation of dropping out, as already noted above.

Returns to Education

One possible reason why youths drop out of schools is that they see low returns to education. But results calculated for this report, as well as results reported in other research, suggest that returns to education in Peru are reasonably high. The rate of return to one more year of education across the entire grade spectrum of the school system was estimated for

Figure 5.4. Grade-specific Enrollment Ratios by Place of Residence

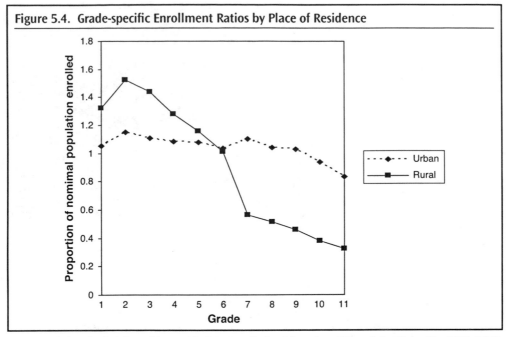

Source: Ministerio de Educación, Unidad de Estadística Educativa, *Cifras de la Educación 1998–2003.*

Figure 5.5. Grade Specific Enrollment Ratios: Impact of Repetition

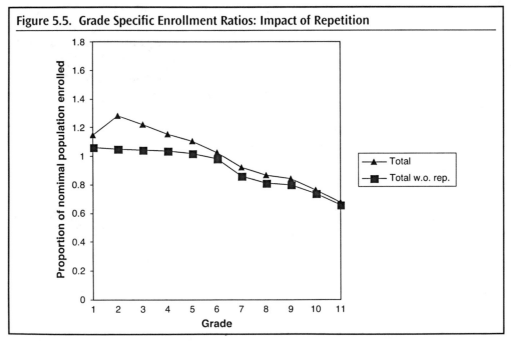

Source: Ministerio de Educación, Unidad de Estadística Educativa, *Cifras de la Educación 1998–2003.*

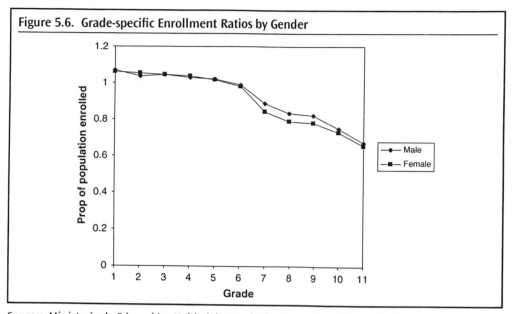

Figure 5.6. **Grade-specific Enrollment Ratios by Gender**

Source: Ministerio de Educación, Unidad de Estadística Educativa, *Cifras de la Educación 1998–2003.*

this report using a simple Mincer model, as 11 percent (ENNIV 2000).[28] Using ENAHO 2003–2004 data, the rate of return for the whole country is also 11 percent (Table 5.2). While it is difficult to establish a strong trend over longer periods, the results from previous years strongly suggest that at the very least the returns have not been decreasing. This is shown in Figure 5.7. Figure 5.8 shows that returns in Peru are on the high side of the international norm.

To understand these phenomena in more detail, both private and social rates of return were estimated by level of education. Three strategies were used: i) the first involved estimating the parameters from a simple Mincer model, ii) the second required adding the interactions of age and education levels to the simple

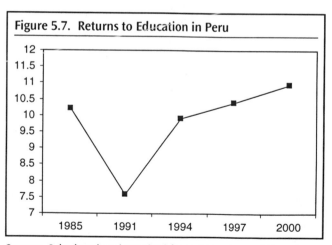

Figure 5.7. **Returns to Education in Peru**

Source: Calculated and graphed from Saavedra and Maruyama (1999) and ENNIV data.

---

28. This estimation was done without data for the Amazon region and for the urban sector only. It also includes only salaried workers in the public and private sectors who work more than 10 hours per week. The ENAHO survey covers all workers and gives the same results.

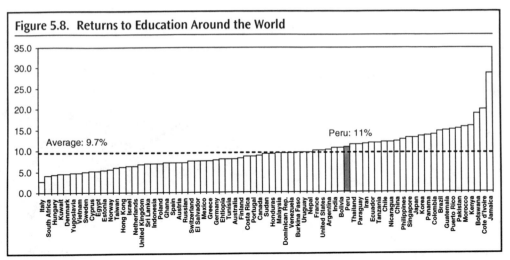

Figure 5.8. Returns to Education Around the World

Source: World Bank/EDSTATS.

Mincer Model, and finally iii) from the household survey, mean wages for each single year of age were tabulated by level of education (minus the mean for the prior level), and their values were discounted and compared to the cost of education. The results show a large private reward for those who finish tertiary education, mainly university. This suggests that even previous levels might have a high implicit return, since completing them is necessary in order to continue on to higher education. It is important to note that the private level-specific returns to *secondary* education, are fairly low, and the social returns are even lower. This could explain some of the dropout behavior that has been observed, and suggests reasons why, when asked why they drop out, youths refer to economic factors rather than the absence of schools nearby. It also confirms the points made elsewhere in this report that further quantitative expansion of the secondary completion rate is hardly Peru's biggest policy problem in education.

Table 5.2. Public and Private Returns to Education

	Secondary		Tertiary	
	Private	Social	Private	Social
Mincer	9.6%	6.9%	20.6%	12.7%
Mincer + Interacted Terms	8.0%	6.3%	16.7%	12.4%
Based on age-wise means	16.2%	10.7%	17.1%	11.0%

Source: Calculated from ENAHO data and per-pupil expenditure data from SIAF (expenditure) and *Ministerio de Educación* (pupils).

Qualitative Analysis of Dropout Motivations

The quantitative evidence suggests that economic problems, poverty, and school quality are important correlates of dropping out (as well as repetition). However, "economic problems" are not a simple issue; poverty is a complex problem that is hard to equate to a mere lack of income. There is good reason to suspect that factors such as school quality, family problems, and economic factors all work together and reinforce each other in complex ways. Furthermore, respondents may be conditioned to give certain answers in response to simple questions in surveys. Finally, dropout behavior may be affected by collective motivations difficult to capture in a survey that, by definition, approaches the problem from the perspective of the individual. Surveys of this nature fail to ask questions whose response may be: "I dropped out because all my friends were dropping out." For this reason, qualitative research was carried out on the social dynamics behind dropout behavior as a means of ascertaining more profound and complex causes, especially around possible collective motivations that imply a "fashion" for dropping out among certain groups of youths.

To assess these deeper issues, focus groups were held with six groups of approximately six or seven youths per group, in three peri-urban and three rural areas (the only areas where significant numbers of dropouts really exist). In addition to qualitative data, some quantitative data were also gathered, though the latter of course represent only a very small and non-random sample. Some of the quantitative estimates nuance the quantitative data already shown above. A few issues are striking.

First, only some 40 percent of these youths lived with both parents, and another 40 percent lived with no parents at all. There is clearly a social and not merely an economic problem—or, rather, the social and the economic are not easily distinguishable. This confirms prior results found by Cueto (2003) and Alexander, Entwisle and Horsey (1997).

Second, the "economic" issue is not so simple. Most (97 percent) of the youths who were working claimed that work did not actually impede them from attending school. Thus, again, what appears as an "economic" problem is not so simple. Working might have resulted in lower academic achievement, however, and this in turn might have contributed to dropping out. The economic and the educational combine—schools may not know how to cope with youths who work. Most of the youths who worked also noted that they would have preferred some form of education that is more closely related to work, and that if this were offered they might go back to school. It is hard to gauge whether this is a conditioned response or wishful thinking, as opposed to revealing a real likelihood of re-enrolling if the right form of education were available. Finally, the youths who were working seldom devoted any of their income to educational or other "constructive" activities. Some of the income was turned over to their families for what are presumably "real needs", but much of the earned income seems to be devoted to entertainment or consumption items hard to associate with "real need".

Third, a notable feature of the lives of the dropouts was extreme general instability of living conditions, particularly in rural areas. A large proportion of these individuals had attended more than one school prior to dropping out. Many had lived in both urban and rural areas. A large number had lost a parent recently, often due to divorce or separation. Many have engaged in petty criminality, associated with gangs, and had discipline problems at school. Quite a few of the dropouts attended schools where dropping out and general indiscipline are known to be a problem. These schools, of course, are the opposite of the effective schools discussed elsewhere in this study. Finally, home life for many of the dropouts lacked direction and warmth. Many dropouts claimed that caregivers had not really tried to stop them from dropping out.

Fourth, a striking finding was the large number of youths who commented on their poor "moral" or "ethical" experience at school. Abuse and corruption (for example, bribery in return for grades, emotional abuse) at the hands of teachers was a common complaint. This was not often cited as a sufficient reason for dropping out, but it often came up as a collateral factor when youths were queried regarding their general satisfaction with schooling. This is not only interesting as a comment on the correlates of dropping out, but as a comment on the education system as such.

Fifth, on the whole (and this went against some of the hypotheses of the study) there is not an anti-school or anti-education culture among the dropouts. At least in terms of the overall discourse, even dropouts claim to value education, and do seem to believe education can lead to better jobs. Thus, there seems to be no sense of a collective culture of disappointment with the quality of education, and there seems to be no overall perception that schooling is of such low quality as to be useless in the labor force. This is confirmed by the quantitative results. The study had hypothesized that at the group level, as opposed to the individual level, there might be a "fashionable" trend to perceive schooling as unnecessary. This generally appears not to be the case, with a few exceptions. On the contrary, dropping out is generally perceived by youths as a form of failure. Speaking for themselves, some dropouts (12 percent) do confirm a lack of interest in schooling as an important factor in dropping out. It is also clear that dropouts seek each other out, lending credibility to the assertion that there is indeed a "culture" of dropouts. But being a dropout is not glamorous, even among the dropouts themselves. The dropouts did claim that among other youths, such as perhaps gang members, dropping out might be seen as glamorous or schooling as unnecessary. Indeed, in the focus groups with youths who were more clearly engaged in petty criminality and who are involved in gangs or gang-like behavior, there is an anti-education culture and a de-glamorization of schooling. However, these youths seemed to be a relatively small minority.

Sixth, the notion of a dropout "decision" is wrong. Dropouts do not actually "decide," in some simplistic behavioral sense, to drop out. Most drift in and out of school, have performance problems, might get into disciplinary trouble, face very bad teachers, have poor attendance, and eventually drift away from school. In this sense, again, economic and educational factors mix and cause each other. The dropout might become disillusioned with school, get a part time job, start earning money and be able to afford status-increasing goods, and start underperforming at school in a spiraling cycle that eventually leads to the complete abandonment of studies. Many of the dropouts, at the time of the interviews, actually entertained hopes of returning to school, though in the judgment of interviewers and focus group leaders, this hope was more wishful thinking than a true hope or expectation. Interestingly, when asked whether school authorities had ever attempted to prevent their drift toward dropping out, only a few of the youths claimed that anyone at school had shown any concern. A methodological implication is that attempting to study dropout behavior using only quantitative models based on the notion of a binary "decision" would greatly under-estimate the complexity of the problem.

Seventh, the qualitative study confirms not only that pregnancy and family problems are the most common causes of dropping out among females, but that these problems also prevent girls from even hoping to ever return to school. While boys seemed to at least entertain the hope or possibility of returning to school, girls were much more fatalistic and appeared resigned to their fate, meaning that they tended to see having a child and taking on the burdens associated with being a mother as a largely irreversible phenomenon. In this sense, programs aimed at dropouts would probably have to contain stronger incentives for females.

Policy Implications

The most clear policy implication is that, at least at the current margin, building schools or adding classrooms is not likely an effective way to ensure enrollment. Other policies are most likely needed. Attention should be paid, however, to the possibility that if other policies succeed, especially in rural areas, a need to create places in schools (by building schools, or adding classrooms and teachers) might indeed arise. Ascertaining the degree to which this might become a problem would require a level of operational analysis, using detailed databases and simulations, that was beyond the scope of this study.

Other policies would thus be called for. Given that poverty factors are the most important determinant of dropout behavior, and that poverty is worst in rural areas, in these areas—and particularly in poor rural areas—a policy of conditional cash transfers, which perhaps contemplates a degree of selectivity for girls, might be called for. However, it has been noted in previous chapters that the quality of education is also a concern: Peru already has an imbalance between access or enrollment and levels of learning; more access and more enrollment would actually increase that imbalance. Furthermore, in this chapter it is also noted that concerns with quality or the relevance of schooling are the third most common reason for dropping out. Because, as was revealed in the qualitative work, motivations are usually quite complex, it is possible that the quality of learning might appear as a more tightly binding constraint if poverty issues were alleviated via a conditional cash transfer system. That is, it should not be assumed that a conditional cash transfer approach could, if it were powerful enough, get rid of all the economic motivations the quantitative analysis documents. Other factors might become binding. Thus, it seems important to address poverty and quality (or interest) issues simultaneously. One idea of potential interest for Peru would be to create some type of cash transfer system conditional on school achievement. One idea worth considering would be a one-time, lump-sum, poverty-targeted payment to those who graduate from secondary school, or, even more interestingly, those who graduate with a "pass" on a secondary-school leaving exam. This would allow the introduction of a secondary-school leaving exam on a voluntary basis at first. Introducing a secondary-school leaving exam might be an important general quality control tool that is unrelated to the dropout issue. Tying such an exam, initially, to a voluntary conditional cash transfer program would be a less controversial way to introduce the notion to society. Care would have to be taken in the design of such an approach, in order to prevent various possible perverse incentives and possible unfairness. It should be possible to create, for example, a substantial prize for last-year students in secondary schools in poor areas who sit for a voluntary exam and achieve the three highest marks in their school, for example. This would remove much of the possible anti-poor bias of a prize system of this kind. It is also likely that the system would act as an incentive for students and parents to demand more accountability from their teachers, reducing teacher shirking.

In urban areas, it seems that other approaches may be called for, although more research would of course be required. Many youths admitted that the level or type of work they do is not really an impediment to further schooling, and most explained that if schooling were more directly useful or interesting, and more related to work, they might consider further study. Thus, it seems as if forms of training that have more direct labor market relevance would be called for. This should not be read as a call for traditional vocational and technical education. Approaches that "voucherize" or somehow subsidize some forms of less formal training, or formal training by private providers (and that also certify this type of training in order to create market information both for trainees and employers), would be worth analyzing in some detail.

CHAPTER 6

Reading in the Early Grades

A Case Study on the Use of Standards[29]

A s noted above, Peru has a minor access and dropout problem, but a major quality problem. The dropout problem was covered in the previous chapter. This chapter turns to education quality, as proxied by poor academic results.

A possible reason for poor results, and for high variance in results, particularly among the poor (a peculiarity much discussed in previous chapters), is a lack of standards of learning and the subsequent application of the same. A lack of standards makes it difficult to program, extract accountability, and design support.

This chapter looks at the issue of standards by first assessing performance on a simple early-literacy task, and then by determining whether teachers appear to be using some standards around early-literacy issues, whether these standards seem to be effective, and if teachers are not using standards or the standards are ineffective, what are the underlying reasons. Similarly, there was a desire to see, if there happen to be some standards (for example, because teachers are following standards that they have received from the Ministry, or they have inherited some standards from their training), whether or not there are support systems aimed at helping teachers deliver to standard.

While the chapter focuses on literacy in the early grades, there is no presumption that this is the only problem. However, it is presumed that the problem of early literacy acquisition is perhaps the most important problem, and certainly a symptomatic problem, because it is probably the easiest area around which to establish standards. If there has been no standard-setting at this level, the problems created by a lack of standards will ripple

---

29. This section benefited from, and is partially based on, the contribution of the consultancy research "Uso de Estándares Educacionales en el Perú," by Marcela Echegaray, Consuelo Pasco, and Jessyca Sampe of TAREA. It also benefits from written input by Helen Abadzi of the World Bank.

through the entire system, and because the system has been unable to deal with this relatively easy task, the failure also symbolizes a generalized inability to set and apply standards.

A tangential motivation for the analysis carried out for this chapter was also to test how much information a well-organized person from, say, a UGEL could get out of a half day visit to a school. The idea here was to see how much quality control (not support) around pedagogical issues a well-organized and concerned UGEL could provide in a half-day visit.

Simple Reading Benchmarks

Reading speed and comprehension were tested as a way to get a fast idea of early literacy acquisition as a proxy for quality of instruction. Methods of introductory reading instruction have been the subject of heated debates, but in recent years many thoughtful reading specialists have converged on what is often called a "balanced" approach to the teaching of early literacy. For example, the National Reading Council in the United States recommends that early literacy instruction include the following components in addition to writing: language and vocabulary development, phonemic awareness, phonics, fluency and comprehension. In this study a measure of oral reading fluency, together with three simple comprehension questions, were used as a proxy for more in-depth reading assessments.

Reading has a strong biological component that has only recently been sufficiently understood. Text comprehension not only depends on correct decoding and vocabulary knowledge, but also on the ability to hold an entire message in short-term memory (or working memory) and process it (Passolunghi, Cornoldi, and de Libero 1999).

As many educators know, the verbal working memory buffer can only hold about 7 items for about 12 seconds (see Reisberg 2001 for a review). If these items are words, then in very rough terms, about 7 words can be kept in memory and processed for 12 seconds at the most. This implies that to be functionally literate, people must be able to read a sentence of about 7 words in about 12 seconds. This frequency amounts very roughly to one word per 1–1.5 seconds or 60–75 words per minute.[30] To overcome this limited 12-second working-memory span, the brain tends to create larger chunks of letters and words and then process these very quickly and automatically. Brain imaging studies show that an express, instant word recognition pathway (in the left occipito-temporal region) becomes activated in the brain as people acquire reading fluency (Shaywitz 2003). Automatic behaviors usually persist, so people who become fluent and automatic readers do not normally lapse into illiteracy.

Thus, reading involves a paradox. Slower readers must make more effort to read, and must muster more attention and take more time. If they do not read a sentence in about 12 seconds, their working memory gets erased, and by the end of the sentence they have forgotten the beginning. It is easy to run out of patience and give up. Children who read haltingly are probably functionally illiterate. They may puzzle out some sentences, but they cannot read or understand the volumes of text needed to learn the curricula.

To activate the instant recognition pathway, practice is needed in consistently pairing sounds with letters. The amount of practice depends on the script and spelling of a lan-

---

30. Reading accuracy is needed along with speed. Small mistakes significantly reduce comprehension because the brain must re-compute the message and thus clutter the working memory. A 5 percent inaccuracy rate in reading is associated with comprehension test scores of only 75 percent.

guage. Most European languages are spelled regularly, and there is close correspondence between sounds and letters. When taught through phonics and in reasonably good schools, children read common words automatically and quite accurately by the end of grade 1. For example, Italian children achieve near perfect mastery of coding skills around the middle or close to the end of the first grade (Harris and Hatano 1999). Spanish is as phonemically simple as Italian. Thus, reasonably fast reading speeds should be expected by the end of grade 1, and certainly by grade 2. More complex transformations require more practice and faster reading for comprehension. A Portuguese-speaking child reading *os mesmos, a gente, bom dia* must understand the meaning at least partly and decide within milliseconds when to pronounce an *o* as *u, d* as *g,* or *t* as *ch.* English and French have complexities that require substantially more exposure to achieve fluent reading. Comprehension in turn facilitates the development of even more fluent reading because people identify letters inside words they know faster than if the letters are seen alone (a phenomenon called the 'word superiority effect'; see Abadzi 2004 for a detailed discussion).

Various countries are starting to focus on reading speed as a simple and practical benchmark in early education. In the United States, proposed reading norms are 30–70 words per minute for grade 1 (oral), 60–100 words per minute for grade 2 (silent), 90–120 words per minute for grade 3, 110–140 words for grade 4, 140–170 for grade 5, and 160–190 words per minute for grade 6 (Barr and others 2002). These data are also available for developing countries. To start with, there are two examples from Chile. First, in the teacher-to-teacher network (red maestros-de-maestros) program of the Ministry of Education (a program where expert teachers, who receive an incentive in pay after they have been certified as experts, reach out to less expert teachers), the importance of reading speed or fluency for comprehension is acknowledged, and goals are set for grades 1 and 2 at 30 and 70 words per minute.[31] As stated on the website, "if children are to comprehend texts, they have to acquire speed in reading. The reading mechanism has to be dominated (automatized). Reading speed can only be achieved one way: by reading." Second, the Chilean NGO *Educando Juntos* has proposed goals around 34 and 64 for grades 1 and 2 respectively, though it is a little hard to discern this from its literature.[32] There is one example from Cuba. In the context of psychological evaluation of children, Cuban expert José Pérez Villar (Pérez Villar 1996) suggests 30 words per minute at the end of grade 1 as a reading speed for a "normal" child, based on simple diagnostic techniques he has developed. It is interesting to compare these possible goals or benchmarks for Latin America with actual achieved levels in Spain, the most developed Spanish-speaking country. There, reported actual averages (not goals) in first and second grades have been found at about 50–55 and about 75, respectively (*Equipo de Orientación Educativa de Marbella 2003*) in one study.[33] Thus, the levels stated as possible goals or benchmarks for Latin America are somewhat below what appears to be actually achieved in at least one case study from Spain. In the United States, using low-income (relative to U.S. standards)

---

31. Sourced at http://www.rmm.cl/index_sub.php?id_contenido=1128&id_seccion=310&id_portal=75 on 13 February 2005.

32. Sourced at http://www.educandojuntos.cl/ on 13 February 2005. Requires drilling down to "Recursos Pedagógicos", "Evaluaciones Estandarizadas", and "Evaluación de la velocidad lectora."

33. The children studied in this case were largely "middle-class" Spanish children, in public schools, typically having had pre-primary schooling of some sort (Personal Communication, Rafael Espada, *Equipo de Orientación Educativa de Marbella,* February 19, 2005).

Spanish-speaking readers of Spanish, the ability to read Spanish at *only* 30–60 words per minute in Grades 1 and 2 has been taken as an index of disadvantage and potential inability to transition into reading English proficiently, and students in this range have been used to test improvement of *Spanish* reading strategies (see de la Colina, Parker, Hasbrouck, and Lara-Alecio 2001). These *at-risk* students were typically reading at about 35 words per minute in grade 1, and around 60 in grade 2.[34] Thus, levels perhaps considered to signal at-risk status in reading Spanish for children in bilingual programs in the United States, are similar to the *targets* or benchmarks for Latin America. And achievement in Peru is considerably below what might be the target for Latin America, as will be seen below. It is to be noted that second-generation Hispanic children in the United States, even if considered at-risk in the U.S. context, are likely to be much more advantaged than an average Peruvian child—not to mention a relatively poor one—in an absolute sense. So, one would expect much better performance for at-risk Hispanic children in the United States than for children in the bottom half of the income distribution of Peru. These sorts of benchmarks can therefore only be taken as a very general indication, and more work needs to be done before firmer ones can emerge. Note though that the analysis in the third section below, which looks at the natural variation within Peru itself as a possible way to establish goals, suggests essentially the same goals that the international literature suggests. Nonetheless, given how modest the standards for Latin America are, they are a good place to begin.

Aims, Method, and Sample

To assess reading ability in children, we decided to concentrate on a simple test of reading speed and comprehension. Children in grades 1 and 2 were tested at the very end of the school year, with only one or two weeks left in the year. A text selected from an area towards the end of the basic, official (and very widely distributed, with coverage being essentially 100 percent) grade 1 language textbook was chosen, and modified somewhat for simplicity and cultural appropriateness to poor schools. The same passage was used for grades 1 and 2 to see whether there was gain in reading ability. The fact that the children may have seen the text before was not judged to "contaminate" the results since there was little chance that the children would have memorized the text, as the nature of the reading task had not been pre-announced, and in any case this was not a high-stakes issue. On the contrary, there was a desire to see whether the children recognized the text, to establish a rough idea of curriculum coverage and textbook use. The text is shown in Appendix A. Similar texts in Quechua (an indigenous language spoken by relatively large numbers of citizens) and Awuajun (an Amazon area language spoken by relatively small numbers of citizens) were produced, again based on official language textbooks, to be used in schools where instruction is (at least in theory) being carried out in these languages. Children were asked to read aloud and were given three simple comprehension questions (also reproduced in Appendix A). The speed was measured, as detailed below. The text length was kept at 60 words, so that for a rather good reader the reading test would take about 1 minute.[35] Children were allowed to finish; they were not cut off at 1 minute.

---

34. Incidentally, the cited study finds that rigorous interventions in reading are capable of quickly and significantly increasing reading speed and comprehension—in a matter of weeks.

In addition to assessing children's reading speed, teachers and principals were queried at each school on goal-setting, standards, processes of pedagogical support available to teachers, and similar issues. Two teachers per school, as well as the principal, were typically interviewed. When possible, one or two parents at the school were interviewed to look into issues of parental involvement and accountability. (This was done on an opportunistic basis.) Finally, classroom observations were also carried out. The idea was basically to see how much information regarding basic abilities, as well as management, and pedagogical issues, could be gotten out of a school in a half-day visit by a single researcher, and to see how much use could be made of the information gathered. The "model" or hypothesis for this approach was to see how much could be done in the time an inspector or advisor might have to visit a school, in a reasonably tightly-managed but resource-constrained system. It was felt that a visit requiring half of a person-day is an appropriate model. This report summarizes and exemplifies what can be done with the information thus derived. (Not all the information is used due to a lack of space and because some of it lacks relevance.)

Twenty-two schools were chosen to be representative of various geographical and cultural groupings in the country (coast, mountains, and jungle areas, urban and rural) as opposed to utilizing a true random sample, though care was taken to prevent obvious biases (such as convenience, or special project influence) from entering into the sampling. However, in order to develop a sense of what could be done in reputedly "good" schools, a few "good" public schools, as well as "good" private schools catering to poor communities, were chosen. Schools were chosen from districts in the poorest two out of five classification groups in the FONCODES (the national social development fund) poverty map, except in the capital city Lima, where it was difficult to find schools in the poorest two classifications, so schools in districts belonging to the third classification were used. One factor that biases the results in a favorable direction (better cognitive development) is that in order to control costs, schools that would have required more than, say, a day of travel time from the nearest form of motorized or boat transportation, were not chosen. Nonetheless, the sample did include highly rural schools that could be reached only by canoe, or after many hours' walk, for example. But the very remotest schools, that would have required a whole day's walk, for example, were not included. Table 6.1 shows the distribution of schools by area and type.

In each school, five children were chosen at random from grades 1 and 2. In total, 245 children were tested. Each child's reading was recorded on a very small, portable, digital recorder (approximately the size and weight of a small cell phone).

Basic Results

The most basic results are presented in Table 6.2.

In this table, "could read" means to be able to literally recognize at least one word (from the first few) in the reading text. Hence, "could not read" implicitly means not

---

35. In languages with compound words, the actual words in the reading were kept much lower than 60, counting the concepts embedded in the long, compound words as if they were words. It is also to be noted that even taking this adjustment into account, the use of compound words could reduce reading speed. Nonetheless, it should not account for children's inability to read a single word, which is what we frequently found in these languages.

Table 6.1. Basic Sample Characteristics for School Reading Standards Survey

Department	Province	District	Poverty Classification (1 is poorest, 5 is least poor)	Number and Type of Schools
Rural jungle				
San Martín	Rioja	Awajun	2	3 standard public schools
Loreto	Loreto	Nauta	1	3 standard public schools
Rural mountains				
Ancash	Yungay	Yanama	1	3 standard public schools
Cusco	Anta	Ancahuasi	2	3 public bilingual schools
Urban coast				
Lima	Lima	Pachacamac	3	3 standard public schools
Piura	Piura	La Arena	2	3 standard public schools
Reputationally "good" public schools (urban coast and rural mountains)				
Lima	Lima	Puente Piedra	3	1 reputationally "good" public school
Cusco	Anta	Limatambo	2	1 reputationally "good" public school
Reputationally "good" private schools (urban coast and rural jungle)				
Lima	Lima	Puente Piedra	3	1 reputationally "good" private school catering to poor children
San Martín	Rioja	Awajun	2	1 reputationally "good" private school catering to poor children

to be able to read a single word. The most impressive fact is, perhaps, that at the end of grade 1, 70 percent of the children in these schools (from the bottom half of the poverty distribution) simply could not read one word. One should note that many of these children have had some form of pre-primary education. Some 84 percent of the children who were asked whether they had had pre-primary education responded "yes." Many

Table 6.2. Basic Results

	Number of Children Evaluated	Percent Who Could Read	Reading Speed (imputing a reading speed of 0 for those who could not read)	Reading Speed (removing those who could not read from the sample)
Grade 1	109	30%	9	30
Grade 2	136	65%	29	45
Total	245	50%	20	41

Source: Calculated by the authors from sample data.

did not respond, suggesting that perhaps they had not had pre-primary schooling, in which case the percentage would have to be taken as 55 percent—a large proportion in any case, and more consistent with official statistics suggesting that about 60 percent of children receive pre-primary schooling. In other words, after approximately 1.5 years of schooling, 70 percent of the children in the bottom half of the society could not read a word. The reading, as noted, was from an area towards the end of the official grade 1 language textbook, yet only some 5 percent of the children remembered having read the text previously. (It is true, as noted, that the text was slightly modified, so this fact should not be taken as overly significant.) Finally, note that a reading speed of only 9 words per minute in grade 1 appears to be way below the relatively modest Latin American standards of 30 words per minute. These results are not too dissimilar from other results known for Peru. In the 2001 National Evaluation, only 34 percent of children in grade 4 were found to have "sufficient" reading comprehension (see Espinosa and Torreblanca 2003). Taking grade 2 children from our sample (since grade 2 is closer to grade 4), and putting the bar of "sufficient" at 60 words per minute (see section 2), we found only 22 percent of classrooms had children reading at that speed or above, but our sample is from the bottom half of the income distribution, so we would expect a number smaller than 34 percent. Other researchers have more casually noted that in many rural schools children cannot read in grades 3 or 4 (López 2002). The table also shows that when children who could not read at all are removed from the sample, reading speed seems fairly high, but this would be an inappropriate characterization of the system as a whole.

An important point to be noted in Table 6.2, though, is that there is a very significant gain in reading between grades 1 and 2. Unfortunately, we did not take measurements on children in grades 3 and 4 (had we suspected the results in grades 1 and 2 would be so poor, we would have taken measurements in later grades), so it is difficult to ascertain whether the gain continues. In any case, it would be reasonable to suppose so.

There are significant inter-correlations (at *school* level, i.e., using data such as that in Table 6.5 below) between these items and reading comprehension (measured as the percentage of children who could answer all three questions correctly). This is noted in Table 6.3.

Table 6.3. School-level Reading Factor Correlations	
Percent reading and reading speed	0.86
Reading speed and reading comprehension	0.82
Percent reading and reading comprehension	0.69

Source: Calculated by the authors from survey data.

More intuitive insight into the relationship between reading speed and comprehension can be gained from Table 6.4.

Schools that simply get children reading also get children to read fluently, and schools that get children reading fluently also get children to comprehend. This may be partly due to some causal relation (for example, reading speed directly contributes to comprehension), or simply because the factors that account for schools doing a good job with reading speed also account for schools doing a good job with comprehension. This suggests that, at least as a baseline diagnostic, checking on reading speed is a reasonable thing to do. However, if no causal relation exists between speed and comprehension (though we have good reason to think one exists), this logic would not extend to either a policy prescription, namely a focus on speed at the expense of other factors, or to a follow-up evaluation of reading projects. In the latter case, a

Table 6.4.   Relationship between Reading and Comprehension

Speed	Number of Children in Grades 1 and 2	Comprehension (average percent correct answers)
Slow (4 to 24 words per minute)	40	26%
Average (25 to 49 words per minute)	39	53%
Fast (50 or more words per minute)	43	86%

Source: Calculated by the authors from survey data. Only children who could actually read are included in this calculation.

diagnostic conducted in a country that had single-mindedly focused on reading speed, or an evaluation of a project that focused only on speed and not on comprehension, might be misleading. In other words, it is possible that the correlation observed between fluency and comprehension in a "natural" or un-pressured setting could disappear in a setting where there was exclusive or naive pressure put on fluency.

The large variability in results is confirmed. The summary or average results above are perhaps useful in raising awareness of the problem, but also tend to mask enormous differences. (And, one must not forget, the averages are not meant to be totally representative, so the variability and the correlations are more interesting than the averages.) Indeed, exaggerating only a little, the system seems to produce results almost at random. Table 6.5 shows results by broad type of school, and, within type, by specific school and grade. In type 1, no children in grade 1 in the three schools evaluated could read at all. In grade 2, anywhere from 40 to 100 percent could read, and the reading speed went from a poor 13 to a respectable 60. These were all schools of approximately the same sociological type. In type 5 (regular urban public schools), we found one school where no children could read at all in grade 1, yet in another 100 percent could read. In type 9, rural public schools in the Amazon area, in one school 20 and 80 percent of children in grades 1 and 2 could read; in the other school, 0 percent in either grade could read even one word. These schools were *not* selected so as to maximize contrasts. It is hard to believe that, say, malnutrition or parental illiteracy could be so bad that not one of the children tested could read at least one word, yet in another school nearby perhaps 80 percent could read. In all, we found that in nine grade 1 classrooms, and in four grade 2 classrooms (out of approximately 22 evaluated), *none of the children tested could read any words at all.*

Finally, and related to the variation, it is to be noted that there are quite a few schools or classrooms that stand out for good performance, which suggests that the situation is not at all hopeless; when a teacher or a school is focused on skills, results can be achieved. In Peru, reading scores are much higher in some standard public schools that have had some NGO assistance, as long as the NGO assistance goes beyond generic management improvement and focuses on very specific classroom management and learning issues. Scores are also high in some schools that have simply decided to apply themselves, and they can be high in some high-quality private schools that serve children in poor areas. Schools or school types 11, 12, and especially 7, are all good examples.

This variation raises important management and benchmarking possibilities. Previosly, we discussed reading speed levels that might be considered useful as benchmarks.

Table 6.5. School-by-School and Type-by-Type Variation in Reading Ability

Type	Grade	Children Evaluated	Percent Reading	Reading Speed	Comprehension[36]
1. Rural, public, Sierra, no NGO or project help (3 schools)	1	5	0	0	0
	2	5	60	32	33.3
	1	5	0	0	0
	2	5	100	60	20
	1	4	0	0	0
	2	5	40	13	50
2. Rural, public, bilingual education, no NGO or project help (2 schools)	1	2	0	0	0
	2	10	100	25	0
	1	2	0	0	0
	2	10	60	8	0
3. Rural, public, bilingual, has health program and school library and texts program	1	3	33	6	0
	2	9	89	17	0
4. Rural, public, Sierra, considered "good", no NGO or project support	1	10	30	4	0
	2	10	50	15	0
5. Urban, public, coast, no NGO or project support (3 schools)	1	5	80	26	50
	2	5	100	66	80
	1	5	0	0	0
	2	5	100	53	60
	1	5	100	39	40
	2	5	100	77	100
6. Public, urban poor, considered "good", receives NGO support	1	5	80	23	0
	2	5	100	67	60
7. Private, urban poor, no NGO support	1	5	100	54	60
	2	5	100	96	80
8. Rural, public, jungle, receives project help in bilingual education	1	4	0	0	0
	2	5	0	0	0
9. Rural, public, jungle, no NGO or project help (2 schools)	1	5	20	4	0
	2	5	80	26	0
	1	2	0	0	0
	2	3	0	0	0
10. Public, urban poor, has some NGO help in health and education	1	5	0	0	0
	2	5	80	24	0
11. Public, urban poor, much NGO and program help	1	5	80	14	0
	2	5	100	52	80

(continued)

36. Percentage of children, out of those who could read, who could answer all three comprehension questions correctly.

Type	Grade	Children Evaluated	Percent Reading	Reading Speed	Comprehension
12. Public urban poor, participate in one Ministry special project (not a learning project)	1	5	60	22	33
	2	5	100	61	40
13. Public bilingual school, jungle, NGO help	1	10	20	2	0
	2	10	30	3	0
14. Public bilingual, jungle, no NGO or project help (2 schools)	1	10	0	0	0
	2	10	0	0	0
	1	2	0	0	0
	2	4	0	0	0
15. Private school, jungle, no NGO or Project help	1	5	20	1	0
	2	5	80	43	50

Table 6.5. School-by-School and Type-by-Type Variation in Reading Ability (*Continued*)

Source: Calculated by the authors from survey data.

This was derived from other countries' experience. One useful (and more easily legitimated) way to set benchmarks is simply via internal reference. The levels of reading speed and comprehension achieved by the best-run schools that cater to the poor, and that have no extraordinary *economic* resources (though they may have had some special pedagogical input) or engage in pupil selection, could be set as benchmarks. The fact that a school may have had pedagogical assistance should not work against its being used as a benchmark, unless that assistance really was substitutive of teacher effort or required extraordinary *economic* resources, because, in principle, once the tools and methods are discovered and well-known, their adoption should not require constant NGO or donor help in *all* schools. Instead, Ministry, DRE, or UGEL systems of in-service training and district—or province-level pedagogical support (as well as pre-service training in universities and teacher training colleges) should, in principle, be able to take care of replication. If they fail to do so, this probably indicates a management and accountability problem rather than an issue of scientific know-how. In this regard, and using our analysis only as an example rather than as a true, valid proposal, a reading speed of some 35 words per minute might be proposed as a benchmark for, say, urban schools in grade 1 (the speeds in the best 3 schools in our sample were 54, 39, and 26, in school types 7 and 5, schools 1 and 2 in the latter), and 70–80 for grade 2 (speeds in the best three schools were 96, 77, and 67, in school types 7, the third school in type 5, and type 6). Note that these benchmarks coincide fairly neatly with those discussed above for Chile—the Chilean scores for grade 2 are a little lower than what is proposed here. These benchmarks are far below what is achieved by middle-class children in OECD countries, and at the level at which Spanish-speaking children reading Spanish might be judged to be at-risk in the United States. A less ambitious benchmark might be chosen, at least initially, for, say, bilingual schools in rural areas. However, the goal should clearly be to reach the same standards in all schools once the models needed for instruction in poorer and bilingual schools are fully developed, understood, and consensus has been reached.

Some Causal Analysis Related to Standards and Support

The method followed and the sample size do not allow for a traditional multivariate analysis. However, by focusing on a few powerful and simple indicators of school processes, one can form some idea of the problems at hand with a particular emphasis on aspects relative to reading and writing. What are some possible causes of both the variability and the apparently low levels of reading? Our analysis attempted to look at some possible issues, though not with the full depth that would be desirable in a more complete and expensive survey. Again, part of the purpose here was to see how much can be done with a fast and inexpensive process that could be duplicated by UGELs and DREs. A few issues stand out.

First, the basic curricular statement of the Ministry of Education does not have very specific goals, and in any case the goals are for the first cycle as a whole (pre-grade 1, grade 1, and grade 2). The statement does lay out the expectation that children should read at the end of grade 1 (Ministerio de Educación del Perú 2000). However, compared to other curricular statements and guidance documents from other countries or other structures within Peru, the goals are rather general and the guidance seems vague, on the one hand, and over-ambitious on the other. For example, in a country where many children are apparently not learning to recognize words at all, even in grade 2 but certainly in grade 1, one of the curricular goals by the end of grade 2 is to get children to "reflect on the linguistic functioning of the texts and systematize their findings to improve their reading and text production strategies" or "to realize that the meaning of the text is constructed while reading, and that it is reconstructed each time it is read anew, because it can make way for new information that modifies the initial meaning" (p.11, our translation). It is difficult to estimate what a poorly trained teacher is to make of such language, or how she is to make use of this guidance in teaching, as it is likely that some of the teachers are themselves incapable of "reflecting on the linguistic functioning of the texts." One can compare the official curricular statement to that of *FyA* (a "chain" of religious schools that function with public support and cater to relatively poor children), for example. The latter provides much more specific guidance and the curricular statement has fairly clear links to an assessment strategy (and the explicit assessment strategy links back to the curriculum)—see Table 7.3. Furthermore, the curricular statement of *FyA* is based largely on an empirical analysis of what is doable and what is done, based on many years of experience (see Alcázar y Valdivia 2005). Similarly, the curricular guidance provided in Chile or South Africa is quite specific (Ministerio de Educación de Chile undated; Department of Education 2002).

The implicit recommendation here is not that Peru should deprive itself of lofty goals and high-level thinking on the cognitive skills children should have, for example, in reading. Instead, the recommendation is that Peru urgently needs to go beyond lofty statements and stop assuming that most teachers are capable of adapting these statements and setting their own standards. Peru needs to specify goals or standards that teachers and teacher trainers find useful as concrete goals and guidance. Thus, the high-level, abstract statement can co-exist with high-quality documents where specific standards, that tie back to the broader curriculum, are presented to the community. Other countries manage to do this, though it takes considerable leadership and consensus-building given that it is the attempt to get specific that brings out differences in points of view. No implication is intended here that having a very specific and clear curricular statement will guarantee good results, since Chile's results are not as far above Peru's as one would expect based on Chile's income per capita, spending levels, and history of literacy—and South Africa's results are worse. Nonetheless, the point is that other countries are concerned with making their curricula as specific as possible and manage to do so.

Second, one might think that teachers do not realize the importance of goals, and do not work with goals. But, interestingly, teachers are at least aware that they need goals or standards. A total of 54 teachers in the 22 schools were surveyed. When asked, almost all teachers (94 percent) said they set specific goals. Whether they actually do, or respond in this manner because they know this is expected, was impossible to tell without more intrusive and thus much more expensive querying. In any case, this possibility does not matter as much as the fact that teachers are aware that specific goals are a good idea. That they may actually be setting goals—rather than simply giving the "right" answer to the question—is suggested (but only suggested) by the fact that when asked how they set goals, and what goals they set, most gave reasonable and specific answers. For example, in answer to the unprompted question "what sorts of goals do you set?" only 28 percent were unable to provide an answer. This may be a large proportion of teachers without goals in some absolute sense, but it is lower than we expected. Finally, most teachers are even able to specify approximately what percentage of children has met the goals, and they themselves realize that they are largely not meeting goals (see below).

It is important to note in these answers that only 41 percent of teachers claim to set their goals in reference to guidance from the Ministry or other education authorities—most use, instead, their own experience or that of trusted colleagues, partly because they consider that the curricular statement is too theoretical, and insufficiently based on teachers' own experience. This is in spite of the fact that most claim to possess and to know the curricular structure (70 and 69 percent respectively), though we were not able to verify this response objectively (e.g., by asking them to show it, or testing them on it). A full 80 percent of teachers, and 95 percent of the principals, considered that the curricular structure is too hard to apply or is inappropriate; 73 percent of teachers considered that the curriculum was crafted largely by specialists without consulting teachers; and 80 percent responded that in their view this is an inappropriate way to formulate a curricular statement. It is difficult or impossible to give objective credence to these opinions—they are indeed largely opinions. Thus, it is difficult to state objectively that the curriculum is indeed "too difficult to apply." Nonetheless, while subjective, these opinions tend to create a sense that the curricular guidance provided to teachers is not very workable or practical, and they do suggest that the teachers' frame of mind with respect to the curriculum is not very positive. Taken in conjunction with a direct textual examination of the abstract and theoretical language of the curriculum statement, and comparing it to that of other countries and of other structures in Peru, one does get the strong impression that the curricular statement in Peru, and the resulting guidance, is simply impractical.

Not only are teachers apparently aware that they need to set goals, but also seem to perceive that their students are not really achieving the goals they have set. According to teachers, only some 55 percent of children have achieved the goals set by teachers. Unfortunately we found a relatively low correlation between how well the children are doing on reading fluency and comprehension and their own teacher's judgment as to whether children were meeting the goals: the correlation was only 0.25 to 0.30.

We have seen that teachers appear aware that goals are a good idea; they claim to have goals and are even cognizant that they are largely not meeting goals. This all suggests that it is not so much a lack of awareness of the importance of goals but instead other ma\ that are contributing to low achievement. These factors could refer to: a) lack of press and accountability to perform to goal, or b) lack of knowledge and support with regard to how to set practical and detailed goals that would put Peru closer to a standard, and how to achieve the goals set. Contextual factors such as poverty and malnutrition could of course also be a problem, but it has been shown (see Chapters 2 and 4) that there seem to be plenty of schools in poor areas that perform much better than others. That is, performance varies significantly even holding poverty and other factors constant.

Because all our reports are based on teacher opinion, it is natural that teachers would not focus on their own accountability in all these matters, and in a survey of teachers it would be largely futile to attempt to assess this issue. Other reports suggest accountability for performance and incentives to perform are extremely low in Peru, as is evidenced by low time on task and curriculum coverage (Cueto, Ramírez, and León 2003; Cueto and Secada 2001). Reports of wasted time are rife in Peru, and what is particularly worrisome is that there appears to be little awareness among teachers and principals that this is a problem (personal communication Richard Webb on work carried out by Elizabeth Linos on August 19, 2005; personal communication Barbara Hunt on work carried out by Patricia Oliart on August 19, 2005). Excessive time for breaks, time wasted on forming lines to enter school, schools making decisions about taking extra vacation, teachers spending time idly chatting with each other while the children are unattended and not on-task, and so forth, are common and seem to create little concern. The current official policy goal of 1000 hours of effective instruction per year is clearly not being adequately enforced, and there are no efficient mechanisms in place for enforcement.

However, some of the factors related to the support issues were striking. For example, we attempted to assess whether teachers receive specific pedagogical support in response to their own perceived—and reported—lack of goal achievement, as opposed to the sorts of generic training that are quite common in most developing countries. The results were quite revealing. Only 13 percent of teachers claimed that they had received support from outside the school. Some 72 percent of teachers responded that there is no specified mechanism for reporting on problems and requesting support. (This could simply mean that, though there is a mechanism, the teachers are unfamiliar with it or report that they are unfamiliar with it. In any case, this is an important fact.) Again in terms of support, only 44 percent of school principals claim to have written goal statements for their teachers as guidance for learning achievement in the early grades. (We did not ask to see the goal statements, so this percentage is probably optimistic.) The quality and orientation of pre-service training was judged by 81 percent of principals to be inadequate for practical classroom work.

It is clear that input supply problems are also at work. Textbooks can be taken as a case in point, given that they are perhaps the most important input. Anecdotal evidence gathered by the researchers suggests that the Ministry's textbooks are not as widely used as they could be. (Further, note that only 5 percent of the children evaluated could recall ever having read the chosen passage, though one should note also that the passage had been altered slightly.) Furthermore, while coverage was very good, the books arrive late. While 80 percent of teachers say they get enough books for all their children (and *all* teachers who responded got *some* books), they also report that textbooks reached them, on average, 9 weeks after the start of the school year. The distribution of the timing is shown in Table 6.6 (the school year starts in early April). In a school year that contains approximately

Table 6.6. Week of Textbook Arrival in the Classroom as Reported by Teachers	
Week of Arrival	Percent
2nd in April	1.9
4th in April	7.4
1st in May	13.0
2nd in May	7.4
3rd in May	1.9
4th in May	5.6
1st in June	22.2
2nd in June	3.7
4th in June	3.7
1st in July	3.7
2nd in July	5.6
3rd in July	1.9
4th in July	1.9
1st in August	1.9
2nd in August	1.9
2nd in September	1.9
Don't know/no answer	14.9

Source: Calculated by the authors from survey data.

36 weeks, this delay implies a loss of one-quarter of the school year. This is not a new problem. When asked how late books have arrived—historically speaking—the claim is that books traditionally arrive some seven weeks after the start of the school year, on average. Textbooks are arguably the most important input in education, after teachers. Thus, performance on this issue is probably a good proxy for overall managerial performance, and it appears sorely lacking (though, as the children actually do get texts, the situation is better than that found in many other countries).

Finally, use of classroom time seems quite poor and below any reasonable standard. Table 6.7 shows the distribution of observations of classroom time use. Two observations were taken on each classroom at different times of day, if possible. About half of classroom time is wasted on relatively low-value activities. (Detail as to what activities were considered "high value" pedagogical activities is shown in Appendix B.) If one adds this to evidence of very low time-on-task from other surveys (Cueto, Ramírez, and León 2003; Cueto and Secada 2001), poor use of time seems an important factor in explaining poor results, and is most likely due to lack of standards and lack of accountability pressure to meet standards.

Table 6.7. Teacher Use of Classroom Time, from Classroom Observations	
Low-value activities	48%
Medium-value activities	40%
High-value activities	12%

Source: Calculated by authors from survey data.

In summary, though the research did not really aim at rigorously establishing the causes for poor performance, the analysis does suggest that either accountability or lack of support in establishing good norms and standards, rather than total ignorance regarding the importance of goals and standards, is an important issue. The results also suggest that lack of *specific* support (for example, support that is responsive to a specific, reported problem, via an established system) is indeed an important reason. (Generic support and capacity building appears to be less of a problem, as most teachers have been trained both in-service and pre-service. Yet, as suggested by the principals, the pre-service training, at least, does not prepare teachers for classroom work.)

An interesting point does come out of parent interviews (unfortunately only 27 parents were interviewed): most parents are quite happy with their children's schooling. Fully 89 percent of parents claim their children's school is a good one. This does not appear to have been a totally "socially expected" response. When queried as to why they thought the school was good, all of the queried parents were able to give a response, and of the 24 responding positively, 9 stated the children were learning well. Furthermore, this is not a result peculiar to our survey, or even to Peru. The 2001 National Evaluation, which has a very large and representative sample, found that, among parents of 4th graders, 80 percent or so (depending on the aspect) were happy or very happy with each of five aspects of schooling. Worse, not only were parents happy in general, but the correlation between children's measured achievement and parental satisfaction with (specifically) the academic level of the school was only 0.26. A similar lack of connection between the rating of the management performance of school managers and parental satisfaction with schools was found in Indonesia. Parents are not only generally happy (more than 80 percent are happy with school processes), but their satisfaction level is relatively uncorrelated with managers' ratings of managerial performance (for example, how long it takes to transfer a child between schools, how long textbook procurement takes) of various districts—these correlations are always less than 0.10 (World Bank 2004). Given that children do not seem to be learning very much, all this suggests parents have rather low expectations, probably due to the lack of specific, simple, communicated achievement metrics or goals. In this respect, it is probably over-optimistic to expect parental input and pressure to lead to quality improvements in Peruvian education, unless standards are first created and popularized and the information on individual school performance against standard is disseminated to parents.

CHAPTER 7

School Management Issues[37]

Behavior and Choice in Peru's Public Schools

Introduction and Method

In many schooling systems, there are failures in the "long route" of accountability. (See Chapter 3 for an explanation of this terminology and the concepts discussed in this paragraph.) These failures are associated with poor quality of schooling, particularly for the poor; this means that there are breakdowns in the accountability of the state to citizens, and particularly to poor citizens (failures of "voice") and failures in accountability of schools to the state (failures of "compact" and management). In these situations, there is often no way for the poor to express their desires so that these desires have consequences; as such, the government can ignore the needs of the citizens, and particularly the needs of poor citizens. Even if government were solicitous of citizens' needs, however, the response would be poor: there are no standards of service at all, or the standards are difficult to render operational, and there is little effective control of schools by the bureaucracy. In any case, whatever standards do exist are not applied—absenteeism is rife, the curriculum is not applied, poor teachers are not supported, disciplined, or eventually dismissed. This is obviously aside from material poverty, because in principle even a poor society can have administrative discipline and can set and keep standards. Instead, in many poor but badly managed education systems

---

37. This section is based on the author's interpretation of "Escuelas de FyA en el Perú:

   Análisis del modelo de gestión institucional y pedagógica y lecciones para la educación pública", and "Prestigio institucional y eficacia escolar en colegios públicos: un estudio de casos en cuatro ciudades del Perú", consultant reports prepared for this study by Lorena Alcázar and Néstor Valdivia, of GRADE.

one finds both unrealistic standards in theory, on the one hand, and very little actual application of any standards at all, on the other. When there are accountability failures in this "long route" of accountability, a fairly common recommendation is for countries to strengthen the "short route" of accountability, both by increasing parental choice over service providers (a "voucherized" approach), and/or by improving direct parental influence via more powerful and localized school councils (an "autonomy" or communitarian model). These are the main recommendations of a typical accountability-based approach, such as that promoted in the World Bank's *World Development Report 2004*. This section explores the degree to which these methods are already at work in Peru, and whether they seem to have much impact. It therefore evaluates whether further "short route" accountability should be encouraged.

This section is based on the hypothesis that considerable choice already exists in Peru's urban areas because there is no effective school zoning and schools are reasonably accessible via public transport. Parents can and actually do choose which public schools their children might attend. It was supposed that such parental choices are guided by reputation—though the reputation might not necessarily refer to academic achievement, since parents value other aspects of schooling, such as discipline for its own sake and the inculcation of moral values in their children, or may even pursue pure snob values.[38] The section further took as its point of departure that, if parents choose by reputation, and if defense of reputation requires certain managerial behaviors, then choice would have behavioral consequences in school management. Finally, it was supposed that these behavioral consequences would tend to be associated with good academic results, or that these behaviors would at least correspond with behaviors which the literature identifies as typical of "effective schools." The policy implication would not necessarily be that more "school choice" is the solution, but that the managerial choices and strategies employed by "schools of choice" would be of interest even to the "compact" aspects. Accordingly, there may be lessons for public sector reform that can be derived from how the "schools of choice" are managed.

To test these hypotheses, this section studied schools that had a good reputation to see whether they in fact had good results or at least defended their reputation with certain behaviors. Obversely, schools that appeared to have good results were studied to see if they had a good reputation, and, again, to see what behaviors were associated with the defense (or buildup in the case of younger schools) of this reputation. The reputation-defense behaviors (if any were found) that appear to be common to these schools were compared against the behaviors associated by the literature with "effectiveness." Due to cost and time constraints, a large-sample quantitative study was not possible. Furthermore, there was interest in deeper insights into how the mechanics of reputation defense work. The methodology employed was to select a few schools, and to conduct focus groups and interviews with school leadership, teachers, and parents. Subsequently, some of the hypotheses were confirmed and others were not—with the qualification that studies using this sort of methodology can hardly give unequivocal confirmation or refutation of hypotheses. The

---

38. Educators probably dismiss these issues in too facile a manner. Parents may seek school characteristics that appear to have only snob or "school spirit" values. But school spirit and identity may have a productive value, as opposed to merely a consumption value, in furthering learning achievement. Thus, deriding parental choice based on school characteristics such as having an English name, or the distinctiveness of the school uniform, is probably unwise.

results are, in any case, perhaps even more interesting than if the hypotheses had been uniformly and simply confirmed.

Only secondary schools in urban areas were studied. This was done not because the study supposes these schools to be more important than others, but because it is typically only in urban secondary schools that choice factors operate strongly and without artificial stimulation. Again, since the policy implication is not necessarily to extend choice everywhere (in the rural areas it may not make sense) but to use either parental pressure or compact mechanisms to extend the behaviors *associated* with choice, this approach is sensible. The idea, for example, might be to assess which behaviors "work" and then to create, in parents living in areas where no school choice is available, a sense that they have a right to schools where these behaviors are common; additionally, parents should be trained in procedures to demand, assess, and enforce such rights. Similarly local education offices (UGELs) would be trained to teach schools how to respond to parental demands with appropriate behavior change.

The process for school selection took into account two factors: "reputation" or "prestige" and objective results. The reputation factors were established via an existing survey of school reputation (which unfortunately covered only Lima-Callao) and via interviews with local experts (such as at the UGEL level) in two other urban areas. Because there was an additional interest in seeing whether reputation and results were correlated, schools were also chosen on the basis of having good results in the 2001 mathematics assessment, defined in two ways: schools that were at or above the mean performance and whose actual performance was higher than its expected performance on the basis of inputs and socioeconomic profile of students (where the expectations were ascertained via a simple OLS analysis). Because the 2001 national assessment is sample-based, one could not always ascertain the objective results of schools with a good reputation; it was possible to determine objective achievement only if schools of reputation happened to fall into the sample assessment sample. Thus, it was necessary to proceed from both directions. That is, in the end, schools that either had a good reputation or good results, or both, were included.

On the basis of these factors, the urban secondary schools chosen are shown in Table 7.1.

Findings

Reputation matters, is known, and choice is exercised. The public can indeed identify and rank schools by reputation. In a Lima marketing survey, respondents were able to identify and rank schools by perceived quality. In the analysis carried out for this report, in which local reputation was assessed less scientifically, it was typically possible for respondents to identify public schools that, in their view, stood out. Thus, public schools are not all the same, at least in the public's eye. Furthermore, schools that have a good reputation have waiting lists and selection mechanisms. Parents from areas of the city other than where the school is located do seek to enroll their children in schools with a good reputation. (However, as will be seen below, reputation is often dependent on signals that may not have much to do with academic achievement. Thus, choice does not necessarily put positive pressure on learning.) The obverse is also true. There are schools known to have difficulties and known to be frequented by youths with behavior problems. It is explicitly recognized by youths and parents that this is not necessarily correlated with the poverty of the youths: some schools are simply places where problematic and undisciplined youths tend

Table 7.1. Schools Chosen for Assessing School Effectiveness Factors

School	Reasons for Selection	Management type	Location Region	Location Province	Location District
Francisco Antonio de Zela ("FAZ")	Actual marks above expected marks and above national average, has reputational prestige in Tacna area	Public	Tacna	Tacna	Tacna (Cercado)
Manuel A. Odría ("Odría")	Marks somewhat above average in spite of low-income students, has good local reputation within the peri-urban area where it is located	Public	Tacna	Tacna	Ciudad Nueva
Nuestra Señora de Guadalupe ("Guadalupe")	Great prestige. No marks available from 2001 assessment, as it was not in the sample	Public	Lima	Lima	Lima (Cercado)
María Auxiliadora ("MA")	Marks higher than average, higher than expected value, and has prestige	Public under concession to religious group	Lima	Lima	Breña
Alcides Spelucín Vega ("Spelucín")	Marks slightly above average and above expected value, reputation weak or indeterminate	Public	Callao	Callao	Callao
Mariano Melgar ("Melgar")	Marks were lower than their expected value and lower than national average. Has past reputation, underwent period of decline, is trying to improve its current reputation	Public	Lima	Lima	Breña
Antenor Orrego ("Orrego")	Marks above expected value and slightly above average, reputation weak or undetermined	Public	Lima	Lima	San Juan de Lurigancho
San Ramón	Marks above expected value and slightly above national average, reputation weak or undetermined	Public	Junín	Chanchamayo	San Ramón
Nuestra Señora del Rosario ("NSR")	Marks higher than the expected value and considerably higher than national average, good reputation	Public under concession to religious group	Junín	Huancayo	Huancayo

to congregate, where such problems are tolerated (causing a cumulative problem of dys-functionality), and there are other schools where indiscipline is not tolerated.[39]

Behavior affects reputation, but enhanced reputation is not always the main motivation for effective behavior. We found that in the schools with both good results and good reputation, behaviors tend to be *different* (though not necessarily effective in academic terms—many of them have to do with extracurricular activities, as will be seen below), and are actually self-consciously different—teachers and parents were conscious that managerial and teaching behaviors are different. However, only in some of the schools is the behavior consciously aimed at preserving or enhancing reputation. In some of the schools visited, and among some teachers in other schools, intrinsic pride, a sense of duty to community (and even abstract duty), and a sense of professionalism all lead to behaviors that enhance reputation, but the behaviors are not engaged in *because* they lead to improved reputation. This was particularly true, as one would expect, in the schools under management by religious groups. It is consistent with the findings on *FyA* schools, reported in Chapter 7. In fact, in only one of the four schools with many effectiveness-related behaviors (Odría), could one argue that the pursuit of an improved reputation was clearly a driver in promoting behavior (and it is not so clear that these are behaviors that actually produce much better results—the point is, though, that there is reputation-seeking behavior). In the other three (Francisco Antonio de Zela, María Auxiliadora, and Nuestra Señora del Rosario), some combination of religious and militaristic or national-pride factors seem to play a powerful role in generating pressure for effective behavior, though in one of them (Francisco Antonio de Zela) there is a combination of intrinsic pride and behavior that specifically seeks to maintain reputation. In the case of intrinsic motivation, the behaviors do generate a good reputation, and generate excess demand for placement in the schools. In this sense, choice is exercised and is consistent with effectiveness. But the directions of the logic and causality in these important cases are the opposite of those that were hypothesized. The hypothesis was that choice is based on reputation, and that the need to defend reputation leads to effective behaviors. The reality appears considerably more complex. Choice is affected by reputation, but reputation is only somewhat correlated with objective factors, and behavior was not in most cases prompted by the desire to create or defend reputation.

Behaviors that seem to be associated with effectiveness and reputation were fairly easy to identify; they cluster, and many are in principle replicable. In order to assess presence of important managerial and pedagogical behaviors in the schools, a more or less standard of "effectiveness" factors was chosen, via reference to what literature already exists in Latin America on this issue (Báez de la Fe 1994; Muñoz Repiso and others 2000; Dávalos 1998; LLECE 2002; CIDE 2003). The following factors were tentatively identified:

1. Clear leadership from the school principal, focus of the principal on teaching quality, pedagogical leadership and support provided by the principal to teachers.
2. Space for de jure or de facto autonomy for the schools, particularly in management of personnel.
3. School's mission and objectives are clear and widely shared.

---

39. The insight about dysfunctional schools was derived from the research into dropouts carried out for this report. See Chapter 5.

4. School is orderly and secure. Norms, policies, and procedures are clearly established and known by all.
5. Discipline in development of school activities, use of positive reinforcement mechanisms for both teachers and students.
6. School is centered on teaching and learning. Time is optimized and time-on-task is high. Emphasis on academics.
7. Stimulation of students is both intellectual and emotional. Teachers have high expectations of *all* students.
8. Teachers actively support the learning of all students, and there are mechanisms to help those falling behind.
9. Classroom interactions between students and between students and teachers are harmonious.
10. There is an emphasis on basic skills (reading, writing, mathematics).
11. There is a culture of evaluation and measurement. There is frequent control, supervision, and feedback.
12. There is team-work between teachers and school management. There is cooperative planning and exchange of techniques between teachers. Supervision and support merge with each other, but both take place.
13. Relationship between the family and the schools is tight. Parents are committed to their children's education.

These factors (though not in this order and regrouping some of them) and a few others were assessed in all schools to see which were present and which were not, and whether this was related to the reputation or the objective results. In addition, we added some factors that are not identified in the literature. The more these factors were present, the more a school was judged to be effective (without reference to reputation or objective performance). As can be seen in Table 7.2 below, there was a break in the number of tallied behaviors between the top four schools and the others. On this basis, four schools were judged to be relatively more "effective" (more exactly, four schools had many more behaviors usually associated with effectiveness) than five others. Schools were then sorted according to the number of behaviors present. In order to cluster or rank the behaviors, a contrast was then created between the behaviors present in the four most effective schools and the others. This contrast is simply the probability that the behavior would be present in the four most effective schools minus the probability that the behavior would be present in the less effective schools. Behaviors were then sorted according to this contrast. Thus, in the table below, both schools and behaviors are sorted: the schools by effectiveness, and the behaviors by how much contrast there is between generally effective and less effective schools. In addition, the probability of observing the observed distribution of behaviors in the four sampled "effective" and five "non-effective" schools is also shown, if there was no behavioral difference between these types of schools in the population. The overlap between behaviors with a contrast of 0.75 or larger, or p-value less than 0.01, is perfect. Because the sample is so small and non-random, it seems wise to focus on behaviors or factors with a p-value less than 0.01, that is, to set the bar on statistical significance much higher than is normal.

A few items stand out, and a few more were somewhat surprising. Among the factors that stand out, the importance of standards and standards-based evaluation, broadly understood, is confirmed. Elsewhere in this report the lack of clear standards in public

Table 7.2. Tallies of Effectiveness Factors

Effectiveness Factors	School										
	FAZ	MA	NSR	Odría	Melgar	San Ramón	Guadalupe	Orrego	Spelucín	Contrast	p-value
1 Vision and objectives clear and widely shared	X	X	X	X						1	0.0020
2 Teaching and learning as the key axis of school work	X	X	X	X						1	0.0020
3 Culture of evaluation, monitoring, feedback	X	X	X	X		X				0.8	0.0098
4 Teachers engage in team work	X	X	X	X		X				0.8	0.0098
5 Motivation and sense of mission	X	X	X	X			X			0.8	0.0098
6 Clear norms and organization	X	X	X							0.75	0.0078
7 School environment orderly and disciplined	X	X	X							0.75	0.0078
8 Support to students falling behind	X	X		X						0.75	0.0078
9 Extra-curricular activities	X		X	X						0.75	0.0078
10 Parental participation		X	X	X	X					0.55	0.0391
11 Autonomy in school management		X	X	X						0.5	0.0117
12 Teacher qualifications	X	X	X	X	X	X	X	X		0.4	0.0195
13 Curricular or pedagogical innovativeness	X	X	X	X	X	X		X		0.4	0.0195
14 Principal's leadership	X	X	X		X		X			0.35	0.0781
15 Infrastructure and materials	X	X	X		X			X		0.35	0.0781
16 Emphasis on basic skills	X			X	X					0.3	0.0586
Total factors present	14	14	14	11	5	4	3	3	0		

Source: Elaborated by the authors from survey data.

schools is often discussed, and the presence of standards in *FyA* schools is contrasted. We now see something similar operating in the effective public schools. Factors 1, 2, 3, and 6 could be said to refer to clarity of goals and goal-oriented behavior and measurement. The relative unimportance of traditional inputs (teacher qualifications, infrastructure and materials) and of curricular or pedagogical innovativeness is to be noted. It has been noted elsewhere in this report that Peru's educational climate is somewhat characterized by unsubstantiated "fashionable" approaches in curricular and pedagogical offerings, and that teachers in the relatively effective *FyA* schools seem to be more comfortable with gradual as opposed to abrupt changes based on fashionable trends. The results presented here confirm this impression.

A few items were surprising. First, the role of extra-curricular activities. In many cases extra-curricular activities provide academic enhancement and are, as such, an element that directly creates academic effectiveness. Even when this is not the case, these activities are part of what parents seek in education; after all, education is not all about academic achievement. But the amount of extra-curricular activity that does not seem directly related to actually creating effectiveness was surprising. Because there are few objective ways to assess and compare schools in Peru on an objective and purely academic basis (since there are no universal standardized testing or public examinations as there were in the past), schools perhaps fill this vacuum by participating in many extra-curricular activities that allow them to rank themselves against each other. Marching in parades, athletic competitions, academic contests or olympiads, winning special projects organized by the Ministry of Education, the percentage of children that manage to enter universities, and the existence of gangs (on the negative side) are all examples of mechanisms whereby schools possibly judge each other and parents judge schools. Some schools devote considerable effort to trying to look good on these aspects, many of which are extra-curricular and some of which have little to do with measurable academic achievement. Thus, this is a "noisy" market. Or, perhaps, it is actually a fairly efficient market, but parents value things other than academic achievement—things such as discipline and moral values for their own sake—to a degree that researchers and policymakers tend to "disapprove" of because they are not seen as directly productive of learning achievement. It may be that because researchers tend to "disapprove" of school products that are not directly related to academic achievement, they tend to regard signaling with regard to those products as market "noise" rather than information.

Second, the role of the principal. In Peru, the principal appears to be mainly an administrative manager and not a pedagogical leader, even in some of the better schools. The role of pedagogical leader falls on the Deputy Principal. In our analysis, schools could be reasonably effective if the principal—at the very least—did not stand in the way of the Deputy Principal and the teachers. In some cases, we found an effective principal but the school itself was not very effective. It is difficult to believe that Peruvian reality would contradict one of the most solid findings from the effectiveness literature. It is likely that where good principals do not exist, in the Peruvian case other structures (Deputy Principals, the teachers themselves) have managed to rise to the occasion, and it may also be that the ineffective schools are dysfunctional in ways that are much deeper than a principal could fix (gangs, political rivalries between teachers).

The relationships between effectiveness factors, prestige in the eyes of the public and the parents, and academic results, are not simple. Furthermore, the relationships between these factors are dynamic and have considerable lags. The correlation between the presence of effectiveness behaviors and actual, measured academic achievement (in mathematics) was only 0.55.[40] Furthermore, while there is some correlation between reputation and effectiveness behaviors, the relationship is certainly not a simple one. Schools such as Odría, which manages to do fairly well even though it is relatively new and in an area of comparatively low socioeconomic status (for an urban school), has only a *local* reputation and modest but better-than-average scores, and yet it displays a reasonably large number of effectiveness indicators. It is possible that over time scores and then reputation will both improve with a lag if the effectiveness factors keep up. Guadalupe, on the other hand, has a much better reputation, but shows very few effectiveness behaviors. (Unfortunately, objective performance indicators were not available.) It is a school that traditionally shaped much of Peru's leadership, but has fallen behind. Similarly, Melgar is a large urban school with a respectable reputation derived from its distant past. Today this school shows neither many effectiveness behaviors nor good results and would not be judged a good school by a professional evaluation even if the public still seems to think reasonably well of it. (In our analysis it was clear that there is an even more recent dynamism at the school and a renewed willingness to deal with problems that apparently have undermined its effectiveness in the past—factionalism among teachers, drugs and gang problems, violence). The case of Odría is an interesting one in that it seems that current effectiveness is fairly new and is the result of a school turn-around that was motivated by a relatively recent crisis or breakdown of relationships between teachers and parents. This is consistent with research on "improving schools" from Chile that suggests that in all of the "improving schools" that were studied, an external impact or crisis was always the motivation for a turn-around (Raczynski and Muñoz 2005). Finally, the issues noted in this paragraph need to be considered in light of the finding reported above, namely that motivation for effective behavior appears to be somewhat intrinsic and does not seek only to affect reputation, and that reputation ensues when behaviors are effective for intrinsic reasons.

It could be that the relatively complex and lagged relationship between all these factors is partly the function of a lack of objective information about performance. As will be seen immediately below, many schools seem to relish having some standards against which to measure themselves, and various forms of competition and score-setting tend to emerge in Peruvian society given that the government does not provide metrics. It is possible that if society and market were more fully provided with performance information, the relationships between effectiveness behaviors, prestige, and results, would be clearer. This issue is important to managers, not just to researchers. The point is not to make these relationships clearer so that educators, sociologists, and economists can understand things better. The point is that with more information the actors involved in the system would see the impact of their actions more clearly, and would thus have more incentive to engage in effective behaviors. In conclusion, Peru is far from having an effectively informed educational market, given that information on the quality of supply is very incomplete. Furthermore, there are many intrinsic-motivation and extra-market factors at work.

Good schools, or those trying to improve, seem to actually relish competition and objective comparisons. Schools, or at least effective ones, seem to seek standards, and where

---

40. Though it should be recalled that at the bivariate level the correlation coefficient is the same thing as the standardized regression coefficient or "effect-size". An "effect-size" of half of a standard deviation, or 0.55, is not small, seen in this light.

they do not exist or are not provided by the government, schools create some standards or benchmarks or participate in benchmarks that are not officially recognized as such. Schools engage in a wide variety of competitive behaviors. The analysis carried out found considerable competitive behavior in athletics, in academic "olympiads," in competitively-awarded grants from the Ministry of Education, in school marching performances in parades, in comparing university placements, and in other types of activities that allow schools to score themselves against each other on quite visible and fairly objective metrics. Among Ministry officials and other educational leaders in Peru, there seems to be a great fear of publishing universal information on school performance. Yet, it seems as if schools actually feel a need to assess themselves and to know how they are doing relative to others.

It was also clear that, at least in some cases, schools engage in these activities because succeeding at them serves an information function. Success creates prestige and sends signals to parents. In other cases, schools engage in activities more out of an intrinsic motivation to excel.

The fact that effectiveness factors are easy to identify but have complex relationships to actual academic achievement has important policy and management-development implications. A managerial implication is that if—based on Peruvian research—more certainty can be achieved on how the various complexities work together so that a more reliable list of effectiveness standards can be reached, it will then not be difficult to tell which schools are behaving well. In effect, it is not difficult to evaluate schools and apply the standards. This means that it is not, at least in principle, difficult to monitor and then manage to standards. But the fact that these relationships are complex implies that more research and observation than was possible in the present report is needed.

Schools with better reputations do engage in selection behaviors. As is the case in *FyA* (see Chapter 7), schools with better reputations do engage in "cherry-picking" or "cream-skimming." They attract children who are more motivated, better prepared, or have more parental support—and are hence easier to teach than children in other schools. And this impacts on their results, which increases the reputation of the school, which in turn makes it even easier to "skim" the best out of other schools. There is, furthermore, a subtle interplay between clarity of goals and mission and "skimming." This sort of skimming is an information-intensive function. If the school's goals are clear and well-known, and imply harder work and more discipline, then more motivated parents and children will tend to self-select into those schools; thus, the schools will have to do less selection and will be in a position to claim that they do not actively select. Thus, having clarity of goals, mission, and values is not only "productive" in that it leads to better results, but is also effective in facilitating the selection of children with certain values into the schools by making it possible for them to *self*-select. But this selection is not itself "productive". Thus, some of the better results in the effective schools are simply due to the fact that they tend to have children that are easier to teach, and some of the behaviors that are "effective" or "productive" also play a role in selection. Methodologically, this also means that it would be extremely difficult to disentangle, in a statistical analysis, which aspects of goal-clarity are truly productive, and which are important because they allow for self-selection. In any case, one clearly cannot improve an entire system on the basis of selection. Thus, caution is needed about how much the whole system could improve if poorer schools were simply to "do what the good schools do."

Policy Implications

A few implications stand out from the analysis carried out in this section.

First, more management research of the sort conducted here should be carried out, with larger samples and by mixing quantitative and qualitative techniques. While the research industry in Peru has produced many useful and interesting "production function" sorts of analyses (see Chapter 2), a shortcoming is that many of these studies have not yet been supplemented by management and institutional analysis. "Production function" studies tend to focus on the importance of certain inputs, and for this reason they are quite valuable, but they tend to neglect the importance of institutions (rules of the game) and management.

Second, given the importance of clarity of goals and coherence of institutional mission, it seems reasonable to keep experimenting, perhaps using more rigorous evaluation methodologies, with various forms of concessions and contract-based management, similar to that seen in the cases of María Auxiliadora and Nuestra Señora del Rosario. Again, realism suggests that, because these schools do engage in selection of students (or students self-select), and do not cater to the poorest segments in Peruvian society (nor the richest, by any means), one should expect possibly worse results than are currently obtained if schools of a similar type do reach out to more average or harder-to-teach students, as would be the case in a process of expansion. This should be taken into account in any evaluation methodology. One possible and simple idea to make evaluation easier is that any and all schools operating under concession should be included in the national learning assessments, by definition. That is, they would automatically enter into the sample.

Third, while more research should indeed be carried out as suggested above, the evidence from both secondary, urban "public schools of choice" as well as *FyA*, as well as the evidence from the weak standards application in early reading in a wide variety of schools, suggests that Peru's public schools need to urgently work on a series of interlinked improvements, to include:

1. Much clearer and more detailed standards and expectations. These could be adjusted by socioeconomic background of students. But more standards and clearer expectations are needed. Regardless of what other, more sophisticated, institutional innovations are promoted, without standards no innovations can work. Furthermore, the greater the variety of experimental offerings that exists, the more pressing it becomes to have some form of standardized evaluation. This sort of assessment is important not just for "scientific" evaluation that devises solutions that are then imposed on all, but to inform an evolutionary or "Schumpeterian" approach to improvement. Without some form of universal standards-based assessment it is impossible to judge, in real time, the results of the experimentation.

2. Within a framework of standards, more autonomy-with-accountability and more insistence on service to communities (by giving communities more power over schools) to allow schools to develop institutional character and mission. Currently schools do have plans, but they are weak and formulaic. At the same time, it should be noted that giving communities more power over schools, in the absence of standards and training of communities to use standards, is unlikely to yield much quality improvement.

3. More measurement and diffusion of measurement results, including the possibility of universal testing in certain grades and the use of results to inform schools as

to how they compare to other schools, and what specific lacunae they have in their instructional strategy.

4. More focus on teaching and learning, with more effective time devoted to academic work, and fewer fashion-led changes in curricular approach—less focus on curricular and teaching innovation for the sake of innovation.

Direct Relationship Between Schools and Community: *Fe y Alegría* and the "Directed Autonomy" Model

Background and Method

The *Fe y Alegría* (FyA) system of Catholic-oriented schools provides a model of both effective compact and of school autonomy oriented at direct service to the community. FyA is a "chain" of privately-run schools managed by the FyA system, but with considerable levels of public funding (most of the teaching force is paid for by the public sector). The aim of these schools is to reach poorer children with an education that is both academically solid and focused on certain values (Constance 2003). The FyA system is a useful case study for three reasons.

First, it is large enough to be considered a true system, even within Peru. As of the writing of this document, the FyA system had 71,500 students, 3,200 teachers, 62 large schools, 4 networks of rural schools with 97 additional schools, as well as a diversified set of technical and vocational venues. This size means that FyA has a scope similar to what a decentralized province-level management body in Peru, the UGEL, would handle. Furthermore, Peru's FyA is part of a large international movement. Thus, the lessons that emerge have *systemic* value, not just school-level value.

Second, evaluations of performance regularly show results better than those in public schools, even though: a) costs are about the same or not much higher, as the system uses teachers paid on the same salary scale as public school teachers, at about the same ratios, and b) the children attending are typically from the bottom two quintiles of the income distribution (Morales y Romero 1998, Alcázar y Cieza 2002).

Third, the FyA "approach" is nearly fifty years old (taking the approach to be the continent-wide approach, not the Peru-specific approach); it has been built up over decades and has stood the test of time. FyA schools started in 1955 in Venezuela, and have spread gradually to much of Latin America (Constance 2003).

The main thesis in this section is that there are both "compact" (management and policy) as well as "client orientation" (autonomy of operations and direct service to community) factors that, in terms of the overall accountability framework used in this report, make FyA schools work quite well. An important sub-thesis is that some of these factors amount to a "zero-sum" game in that they would not be replicable to a whole system even if the whole system were privately managed: they only work in a set of relatively good schools that are part of a larger, mediocre system, be it publicly- or privately-managed, and where those schools that are relatively good can "cherry-pick" from the mediocrity around them. For example, better teachers (such as those willing to work harder) will tend to be attracted to better, more demanding schools. In this sense, these schools work better not just because they have better systems but because they have better inputs. In fact, the other schools then get stuck with the worst teachers. Thus, a whole system cannot improve via

these sorts of zero-sum games because by definition a whole system cannot have "b
teachers than someone else. There is no someone else, so the system as a whole has
teachers it has. Thus, these are factors that are replicable but only to sub-systems. There is
a second set of factors that are not replicable at all, at least not at the cost at which FyA provides services, because they are in inherently limited supply. Finally, there is a third set of
factors that is replicable to the scale of the whole country, either to a reformed public system or to a system based on private administration. This last set of factors is the most interesting, so we start with these. An exploration of the non-replicable factors might appear
somewhat academic, in that there might appear not to be any lessons to be learned. Nev-
ertheless, it is important to at least touch upon these points so as to prevent excessive or
naive optimism about the lessons that FyA might contain for the public sector or for mass
replication via private management.

The methodology followed in this section consisted of: a) a review and compilation of
the empirical literature, particularly that which refers to the Peru FyA schools, for basic
background and evaluation of results; b) review of FyA's own documentation; c) focus
groups and key-informant interviews. With respect to the latter, three schools were visited,
chosen from those that were not the oldest and were in relatively poorer areas. Though FyA
generally establishes schools in poorer regions, since that is its mission, some of the regions
served have developed over the years, and parents today in some of theses schools cannot
be said to be poor. At each school the director and sub-director were interviewed, and a
focus group with teachers was carried out. In addition, officials from the head office were
interviewed. All interviews were structured via questionnaires aimed at testing specific
hypotheses and exploring specific questions. The basic hypothesis was that, as noted above,
there are some factors associated with FyA's success that are most likely replicable, and
some that are most likely not replicable. The interviews were aimed at ascertaining the presence and relative importance of replicable *versus* non-replicable factors.

Replicable Factors that Account for Fe y Alegría Success

The analysis of FyA suggests that there are several factors that account for its success, and
that these factors could be replicated broadly; they are not "zero-sum" factors. These are
discussed below. In each case, we evaluate the probability that they could be replicated in
the *public* sector. If they are not replicable in the public sector, the implication is that further experimentation of non-public management but with public funding should be
attempted. Each of the conclusions below is driven by our interviews and focus groups. In
a few cases there is a discussion of these factors in the literature. In general, however, our
hypotheses have not been explored in quite this way (an accountability orientation), so
there is not much literature.

A culture of action, reflection, and evaluation that is part and parcel of Jesuit tradition.
The FyA system originates in the Society of Jesus. This Catholic order is well-known for an
approach to action based on one of the earliest "systems" of what would today be called
"quality control feedback loops", but which is deeper than that phrase implies. The
approach involves a repeated sequence based on the concepts of context, experience, reflection, action, and evaluation in a constant feedback loop (The International Centre for
Jesuit Education 1993; Kolvenbach 1986)—an approach that is applied both to individual
improvement of learners and teachers, and to system improvement as well. While the

Society of Jesus may indeed have been one of the first "Western" institutions to explicitly apply this sort of evaluation loop, by now almost any "rational" and goal-oriented organization that is effective is run in this fashion. The approach is thus replicable within the public sector of Peru, but would require continuity of leadership and resources for the operation of such a system. Yet, these systems are not "natural." On the contrary, they require organizational effort and discipline. Thus, another requirement is the existence of a strong motivation to even consider a system of this nature. In a religious order such as the Society of Jesus, and by implication in FyA, this motivation is intrinsic. In a public service, the motivation has to be external and based on accountability to the public. The latter is not currently operant in Peru's public sector, but it could be generated over time.

Clear goals and sense of mission. A clear orientation around fundamental values of hard work, achievable academic goals, practicality, and devotion to duty and community was widely cited by those interviewed as keys to FyA's success. The literature also highlights this factor (McMeekin, Latorre, and Zeledón 2001; Lazcano 2003; Reimers 1993). This is a very well-known factor in the effective schools literature, so we do not emphasize it here.

Academic accountability appears to be fairly high, though pressure in this direction is not obsessive. The Head Office applies achievement tests every two years. Unlike in the public sector, where results are not distributed to schools or used in any way for specific-school improvement, FyA distributes results of tests back to schools and teachers. However, each school receives only its own results. In the public sector the test results are used (in theory more than in practice) to re-shape pedagogical and support approaches. Because the tests are sample-based, and are in any case not distributed to schools, the test results cannot affect specific schools' practices. No experiments have been carried out in using the tests to feed back quality information to public schools, even on a sample basis. In FyA, the results are known to the schools. Problems and lacunae in pedagogical practice suggested by the tests are discussed and solved. None of our informants seemed to have any great concerns with perverse incentives created by this practice, such as "teaching to the test." FyA seems quite able to use these results with maturity. Whether this would be possible in the public sector is unknown. In any case, because other forms of accountability in the public sector are so much weaker, it may be wise, if such universal testing were to exist in the public sector, to raise the stakes somewhat above the level one finds in FyA (for example, tell schools how well they do in comparison to other schools). FyA has very strong collective and bureaucratic accountability and information mechanisms aside from the testing, so the test results themselves do not have to play a role in accountability; they are used more as information in bureaucratic or "compact-based" quality control feedback loop.

Use of an accretion model rather than a discontinuous reform model. A corollary of the first factor above (a quality control feedback loop that operates constantly) is that FyA has improved its pedagogical and administrative systems gradually. There are relatively few discontinuities such as "curricular reforms" that imply that a previous approach is to be radically substituted by a new one. According to interviews, a serious problem with public schools is the constant change of fashions and approaches. The FyA approach to pedagogical and curricular models is, on the contrary, fairly stable and based on accretion. An accretion model is in principle replicable to the public sector, but is less likely there given that even in a well-managed public sector, bureaucratic fashions are almost inevitable due to the pressure on each successive administration to prove it is taking action. Because the average tenure of Ministers of Education in Peru is eight months, schools tend to be subject to considerable changes in direction. In addition, there is a tendency in the public sector's curriculum to over-reach in terms of explicit pedagogical ambition. As a result, no curricular (or other, but the problem is worst in curricular approaches) reform is ever complete, teachers are confused, too much is expected of teachers in theory (and too little in practice), and it is difficult for teacher training systems to catch up to curricular fashion (assuming they faced the accountability pressure to do so, which is not often the case). In reality, then, pedagogical change in the public sector is incremental anyway, given that this is the only way that teachers can cope. In this case, however, "incremental" is synonymous with "contradictory" and "confused." In FyA the change seems to be gradual, rational, and fairly complete. Private management of public schools, or private management in general, would typically be able to sustain a gradual-improvement model more than the public sector (in Peru, for now) could.

Specifics of curricular and pedagogical approach. While FyA has to use the basic public curricular approach, FyA has refined the approach to make it more practical. In particular, the government's curricular approach, while having certain positive aspects, was seen as not providing sufficiently clear guidance. Competencies and sub-competencies that were supposed to be achieved in the government curriculum were neither sufficiently well-specified nor grade-specific enough to fit what FyA teachers felt was appropriate. Finally, the curricular approach in the public sector was not organically linked to a student evaluation approach. FyA worked on these aspects and linked their curriculum and specific competency statements to means of evaluating whether students were achieving the competencies. In the government sector the curriculum, evaluation methods, and teacher training approaches continue to be disjointed and general. According to the FyA teachers interviewed, the adaptations they have made to the curricular approach make it easier to plan over the year. The curricular approach, furthermore, can be adapted to each school, in that different specific abilities are stated, and different time frames to achieve them might be allowed, but it tends to retain specificity, in that specific ability development goals exist and are tracked.

In this respect, it is interesting to compare the curricular specifications of the national, official curriculum with the further specification of the FyA approach, as in Table 7.3. The official curriculum is, on one hand, ambitious and convoluted in a country where children are taking years to learn to read, and on the other hand, non-specific as to grade or level of ability. The FyA curricular statement is more modest yet more specific (for example, competencies are listed by grade).

Though even the table above is telling in the convoluted language ("constructs the comprehension"), the official curricular statement is even more ambitious, and at the same time vague, than the table above shows. For example, one of the skills children in the first cycle are expected to achieve, in a country where many children in this cycle are not reading any words at all, is: "the ability to reflect on the linguistic functioning of the text . . ." and this is to be tracked by things such as whether the child "is acquiring consciousness that the meaning of the text is constructed as the text is read and is re-constructed, each time it is read anew, because it allows for new information to be added to the sense given it initially" (MINEDU 2002). This mixture of high ambition combined with non-specificity is generally absent from FyA curricular materials.

Furthermore, as noted above, the Head Office constantly evaluates how the teachers are implementing the overall curricular approach, and makes modifications to it based on these evaluations.

Table 7.3 Official and *FyA* Curricular Statements Compared

Official Curricular Statement: Abilities and Attitudes at the End of the 1st Cycle (1st and 2nd grades), Given Jointly for the Whole Cycle[41]	FyA Curricular Statement, by Grade
◆ Constructs the comprehension of the text being read by: 　√ Anticipating the type of text and the purpose of the writing, according to context (situation, motive circumstances and the means whereby the text arrives at his hands). 　√ Reads individually and silently; identifies signals and cues such as: title, subtitles, shapes, known words. 　√ Formulates hypotheses (suppositions) about the meaning of the text. 　√ Tests his or her hypotheses against those of classmates and draws conclusions. 　√ Creates a synthesis on the meaning of the text. 　√ Confronts the constructed meaning with the reading of the text, as carried out by the teacher. ◆ Reads with pleasure self-selected texts: poems, stories, jokes, comic strips, etc. ◆ Reads diverse texts: stories, legends, poems, recipes, letters, cards, posters, news in line with his or her purposes and the needs of the moment. ◆ Recognizes and can classify, according to function and profile, different types of text such as posters, recipes, cards, advertisements, etc. ◆ Can read and use double-entry tables of use in daily life (attendance charts, responsibility charts, achievement charts).	**First grade** • Reads audibly. • Pronunciation is adequate. • Reads individually and in groups. • Reads in groups following models for tone and rhythm. • Respects exclamation and question marks. • Does not sound out syllables. • Reads short (3 paragraphs) texts fluently. **Second grade** • Adapts tone of voice according to audience and type of text. • Respects commas and periods. • Does not sound out syllables. • Does not change letters or words. • Does not add or remove words. • Does not skip paragraphs. • Reads without difficulty words up to four syllables. • Reads short (3 to 5 paragraphs) texts fluently.

Sources: MINEDU (2000); *Equipo Pedagógico Nacional de FyA* (2003), our translation.

Finally, the Head Office also works as a sort of consulting group. Schools or teachers that are having problems know they can request a consultation from the Head Office. In other sections of this report we have documented that teachers in the public sector tend to feel that there is little that a UGEL, for example, can offer by way of specific problem-solving help in curricular and pedagogical matters. The fact that the Head Office is reachable when there are problems means that they tend to detect problems quickly, and feed the problems back to the officials who develop and improve the pedagogical approach.

---

41. It should be noted that the official curricular statement does say that "It is expected that by the end of 1st Grade, children will be able to read and produce texts, and that in 2nd Grade they will consolidate these skills". But this is still relatively vague as to how to gauge these skills, and is found in a section on teaching methodology, not in the main section on expectations.

Having a curriculum with somewhat different progress and evaluation milestones generates some problems for FyA, which have been resolved by generating tables of "equivalences" between their indicators and those in the more general public curriculum. The fact that FyA appears to go through this extra effort signals the value they attach to having their own, more specific curriculum.

Having a well-specified curriculum is in principle replicable in the public sector. Other countries such as Chile or South Africa have made significant progress in making curricula more specific. South Africa is no less diverse than Peru, had a similarly complex curriculum, took stock of the problems this created within a few years of its creation, and changed it quickly. However, this willingness requires that the government be fairly strong and able to steer very capable processes to generate consensus around specifics. Vagueness in the official curriculum appears to reflect both a particular pedagogical approach, as well as difficulty in reaching compromise around specifics. Achieving specific standards requires more technical skill, as well as more skill in driving consensus-building processes, than simply leaving things unspecified. The policy implication on the government side is that more concentrated application of time and talent to curricular improvement is still needed.

Financial autonomy. FyA schools are able to gather and use extra resources in very flexible ways (Swope and Latorre 1998; Romero and Cáceres 2001). These funds originate in both the community of parents and the society at large. Because the management is trusted by parents (partly because of its religious orientation), the ability of management to use funds in a discretionary and flexible way does not seem to create the sorts of problems that are observed in public school APAFAs, where there are constant tensions over financial accountability. This aspect would in principle be replicable in the public sector, if there were reforms in how schools are funded, in how accountability is managed, and in how school directors are trained to be accountable. However, while this might increase parental happiness with contributions, and thus might generate more financial inputs to the schools that may in turn increase efficiency, it should be noted that FyA schools are able to attract corporate and NGO resources precisely because they are islands of quality in a sea of mediocrity. If public schools improved sufficiently, FyA schools would not stand out, and would not receive so many extra resources. On the other hand, based on our interviews, what matters with FyA funding is not only the extra resources they receive, but perhaps just as importantly the fact that these resources are sought and used in a very entrepreneurial fashion. As such, their impact, at the margin, is high. A similar autonomy-with-accountability model in public schools could generate the same kinds of flexibility if the regulations were clear, accountability sufficiently strong, and parental training sufficiently deep.

Staffing autonomy. FyA schools have considerable leeway—in some countries more than others—in selecting school leadership and teachers. In Peru, there is leeway in selection of directors and teachers, but not as much as in Ecuador or Venezuela, where FyA has complete discretion in hiring and firing (Swope and Latorre 1998; Martiniello 2001).

The conclusion of the analysis is that the staffing autonomy results in better control and supervision as well as better on-the-job training, but does not seem to result in much privileged selection on observable variables. While a case study of this sort evidently cannot control for selection issues econometrically, the research specifically tried to assess observable differences which might suggest that FyA schools are picking from a visibly better pool of applicants, simply by asking whether this selection takes place formally or appears to take place informally (for example, better grades at university). The conclusion was that there are few, if any, such characteristics. One possible observable difference is that FyA's teachers tend to be younger, which goes along with a hypothesis that the system shapes rather than cherry-picks teachers (Alcázar and Cieza 2002; Navarro 2002). In the interviews with teachers, most of them said that when they joined FyA they did not sense that they were in any way different from their peers who joined public schools, but that they had been *shaped* by the FyA approach into becoming better teachers. A training or shaping approach is replicable, whereas a cherry-picking approach is not.

To replicate these factors in the public sector the "teacher career" would have to be reformed in drastic ways (significant reforms were being proposed as of the writing of this report), so that the career and system of human resource management could shape teachers. The influence of schools (parents) and directors over teacher careers would have to be increased. This would in turn require much more skilled school directors and parent committees. The motivational factors found in FyA are unlikely to be at all replicable in the public sector.

A "head office" that sees its role as one of servicing autonomous units, the latter having the main "client interface." Each FyA school creates its own pedagogical approach, subject to the overall FyA approach, in order to serve the specific community where it is located. Furthermore, the FyA head office sees each school as the defender of the image of the system, and as its principal interface with the community. This creates pressure on each unit to internalize its quality mission, and creates bottom-up demand from each school for the services of the head office. It also puts pressure on the head office to provide services that are practical and applicable, as opposed to control-oriented and theoretical (Swope and Latorre 1998; Romero and Cáceres 2001). This approach is in principle replicable in the public sector bureaucracy, though it would require drastic changes in orientation and evaluation; accountability approaches would have to be turned around completely in many respects. For example, local education offices (UGELs) would have to learn to be accountable and of service to schools, and schools to communities. Furthermore, while in FyA this approach is intrinsic, in the public sector more extrinsic and hence bureaucratic or market-based approaches would be required. For example, each school could be made directly accountable to its community. The UGEL would then service the school, each school would be required to evaluate the service of the UGEL, and schools' evaluations would have to be taken into account in the evaluation of the UGEL's personnel and its directors' contracts. This approach is allowable in the evolving Peruvian legislation, as this legislation tends towards school autonomy and parental rating of schools. But the vision is at this point very timid and incipient, and none of the necessary systems have been thought out adequately, much less implemented. Pilot experimentation with much tighter and bottom-up accountability is urgently needed.

Control tools are developed based on observed teacher and principal practice, tend to be practical and approved-of by teachers and principals. The above is not meant to imply that FyA lacks quality control tools and systems. On the contrary, each school must have standardized tools such as a School Curricular Plan, an Institutional Development Plan, and Internal Regulations. There is a daily observational protocol ("ficha de observación" or "ficha de acompañamiento"[42]) used by the school director and sub-directors to monitor

---

42. The fact it is often called a "ficha de acompañamiento" ("support or accompaniment form") is revealing of the fact that in FyA control and support functions are well-orchestrated.

teacher work. However, these approaches and tools are based on observation of good practice, and are typically approved by teachers and principals. Because they are based on practice and are built-up over time based on observation of how they work, they tend to actually work; consequently, these tools and approaches tend to make life easier for those who have to use them, so they use them. This approach is replicable to the public sector, but would require continuity of management and approaches. It is more easily replicable by privately-managed groups of schools in the sector, where continuity of management is more likely. Furthermore, the head office does not shy away from control functions. Visits and inspections can be unannounced, but since their results tend to be practical and usable, they are generally not seen as an imposition. A system of random control and support inspections in the public sector is possible, but because: a) schools' goals are vague and are not focused on client service; and b) technical ability in the UGELs is very thin due to turnover and lack of technical training, inspection visits are unlikely to be focused on practical issues. Because inspections are likely to be impractical, they are likely to be resisted. However, this could be improved via obvious reforms in the public sector.

Well-paid management. FyA school directors receive double salaries: one from the Ministry and one from FyA itself. This is easily replicable in the public sector with relatively minor reforms (Alcázar and Cieza 2002).

No factionalism. One of the factors most commonly mentioned by teachers and directors in our interviews was the absence of factionalism within FyA schools. In the public sector, (large) schools are riven by internal divisions and power struggles. Groups of teachers oppose the director, while the director is backed by other groups of teachers or barely subsists if most teachers are opposed to him. Accusations of corruption, power abuse, and legal processes against directors are extremely common, and turnover is high. In FyA schools teachers are united behind a common goal and under the clear leadership of the director. This sort of unity is in principle replicable to the public sector, but in practice it would be difficult. Teamwork requires common goals; teams coalesce around clear and common goals. In the public sector, this would require a much more thorough-going goal orientation than currently exists, greater pressure to achieve the goals, and more capable and trained directors willing to lead through superior capacity and self-confidence as opposed to authoritarianism. Goal- and standard-setting in Peru is very weak, as there is a failure of collective action in the specification of clear goals in the curriculum. Goal-seeking behavior would also require that while directors win respect for superior knowledge and skill rather than authoritarianism, they do have unambiguous authority over teachers. Finally, improving team-work in schools would also require that the education sector not be used by political parties for patronage and organization purposes. In this sense, reforming this aspect would require reforming the public sector as a whole—a very tall order.

Non-Replicable (or less replicable) Factors

FyA also relies on certain factors that are inherently non-replicable to any whole system, whether public or private. They are factors that are related to self-selection, active "cream-skimming" or "cherry-picking", and the use of resources that are inherently in fixed supply. These factors are of considerable importance, and they need to be noted in order to prevent excessive optimism about the sorts of changes that could be brought about via more private management of the FyA type.

Some pre-existing community support. FyA generally operates where there is community support, and typically does not start with an obligation to provide a universal service regardless of the level of community support. The public sector, because of its "universality" mandate, cannot do this, by definition. On the other hand FyA schools actively generate community support. This aspect would be replicable, and is one of the factors shaping the new education legislation in Peru.

Furthermore, in areas where there are existing FyA schools, there is some selection of parents and students based on parental commitment to the school. This selection is accomplished quite easily. To be an FyA parent simply requires much more participation, so only the more devoted parents tend to self-select into FyA. There is a rather daunting list of activities that are required of parents. Thus, no explicit esoteric "participatoriness" evaluation has to be given to parents; the ones who are daunted by these sorts of requirements would simply tend to look elsewhere. Again, schools in the public sector could require (and generate) more participation from parents, but they would not get it as easily, because they would have to work with average parents, whereas FyA, precisely because it is not the whole system, can "cherry-pick" parents who are pre-disposed to be active and support their children.

Nature of leadership. FyA school directors are often foreign and come from a religious background. They have sometimes had experience managing large organizations, even large educational organizations, in developed countries. Their approach to management, and their general attitude, is thus quite modern and sophisticated. In addition, it is values-centered; it is conceived of as something more than "management." This then represents a "factor of production" in FyA schools that is in inherently inelastic supply. On the other hand, not all of their ability is based on deep background issues, and *some* of this ability would in principle be replicable in the public sector if school leaders were empowered to actually manage. Nonetheless, based on our interviews of FyA directors, it is quite evident that the overall caliber and value-centeredness of the leadership is largely not replicable, even if some of the more mechanical management techniques they use are replicable. The average public school director in Peru will, by definition, not have had, in his or her background, the experience of running a well-managed Canadian or Spanish vocational school, and will typically not have the intrinsic devotion to principle that many of the FyA managers have.

Teacher selection. FyA openly selects teachers who are motivated and appear to be hard workers. These are non-observable factors, but they seem to be operational to some degree. Staffing autonomy, which allows selection to assess these factors and "values" more broadly, would be much more difficult to replicate in the public sector and virtually impossible if the sector maintains its current configuration. Furthermore, because FyA selects the most motivated teachers via a "cherry-picking" process, this practice would appear to be non-replicable to a public system. However, Peru currently has a surplus of trained teachers who are not working, so selection, even in the public sector, would be possible. Many of these unemployed teachers may be more motivated than teachers who are currently employed. Anecdotally, one knows that many current teachers have been appointed through patronage processes and are therefore not particularly motivated or well-suited to be teachers. Thus, the public sector could, at least for a considerable time, replace unmotivated personnel with (potentially) more motivated personnel who are currently unemployed. FyA's practice, viewed in this light, is indeed "cherry-picking" but it is a replicable sort of "cherry-picking" because of the particular circumstances in Peru, namely the teacher surplus. Furthermore, one has to note that many of the FyA teachers, as stated above, feel that they were not any different from other teachers when they joined FyA, but that FyA has changed them. Thus, how much "cherry-picking" there is, as opposed to subsequent shaping of those who are chosen, is not totally clear, though there seems to be some.

Policy Implications

There are about a dozen factors that seem to account for FyA's success. Of these, some 70–80 percent are potentially replicable to a whole system, while some 20–30 percent are "zero-sum" factors that by definition tend to be difficult to replicate or, more strictly, that if replicated could not produce better results. The latter are very important, though, so their weight is probably greater than is implied by the fact that they constitute only three factors out of approximately twelve. While this is difficult to measure, one could conclude that the non-replicable factors account for about 50 percent, or somewhat more, of performance differences. Of the factors that are replicable to a whole system, a few would be relatively easily replicable to the *public* sector even with current legislation and norms, though skills would have to increase (for example, improving the specificity of the curriculum, developing better standards that allow linkage of curriculum to assessment). The needed skills are probably only required at the apex of the system. The rest of the improvements would require quite significant reform and expenditure in massive capacity development (for example, in teacher career systems and human resource management, or in school accountability to parents). A few factors (such as decreasing factionalism and personal and party politics in schools) are in principle amenable to reform in the public sector, but in practice are nearly impossible to reform until the public sector as a whole is reformed. Thus, of the ten or so factors that would be replicable to a whole system, most would be replicable to a whole system only if this system included groups of privately-managed "franchises" or "chains." Most of them would be difficult to replicate to the public sector, particularly with the current laws and incentives. This section would thus suggest that further managerial and accountability improvements are needed in the public sector. It also suggests that more experimentation with private or religious management of schools, but with a public funding subsidy base, should be carried out. The areas in which the public sector could learn fairly easily are:

a) Clearer curricular and achievement standards. Less convoluted and esoteric curricular statements.
b) More monitoring and evaluation, and tighter integration of monitoring results into support and standards.
c) More continuity in leadership at all levels; more reliance on accretion and less reliance on curricular and pedagogical "reforms".
d) More use of universalized measurement as feedback to individual schools.
e) Realization that schools are the ultimate quality interface with the clients, and thus more downward accountability and service standards, of schools to communities, of UGELs to schools, and of the Ministry to both UGELs and schools.

CHAPTER 8

Progress and Paralysis on Intercultural and Bilingual Education

A Special Problem with Standards[43]

The Issue

Inter-cultural and bilingual education (EIB henceforth, for *Educación Intercultural Bilingüe*) is not a theme that fits easily into the accountability framework being used in this report. In some respects, it could be framed as a matter of accountability to parents and communities. However, we have chosen to view it as an issue related to standards and the adequacy of pedagogical models, as well as financial, policy, and technical support. That is, we have chosen to treat it as a "compact" issue. The reason for this is that progress in EIB might be conditioned by an important paradox that has perhaps not yet been sufficiently discussed in Peru—the need to standardize and unify the less-dominant languages for teaching purposes, and to create standard pedagogical practices oriented at learners from communities whose mother tongue may not be Spanish. How to create *standards* that accommodate *diversity*, not just Spanish-Indigenous diversity, but diversity of variants of a single Indigenous language group, is a paradox—or an apparent paradox—whose resolution would be helpful in advancing EIB.

The importance of bilingual education in Peru is given by two factors. First, some 26 percent of children have a language other than Spanish as a first language (as determined by the answers of 4th grade students in the 2001 National Evaluation, probably the most reliable source on this theme). If one reasons at the school level, in the average school 31 percent of children have a language other than Spanish as a first language (the difference between the child-level value and the school-level value is due to the fact that schools frequented by chil-

---

43. This section is partially based on the author's interpretation of "Educación Intercultural Bilingüe en el Perú: Tendencias" a consultancy report prepared for this study by Lilliam Hidalgo Collazos and Ingrid Guzmán Sota of TAREA.

dren from non-Spanish-speaking households are smaller). Second, there is a significant correlation between having Spanish as a first language and school achievement. The bivariate correlation between being Spanish-speaking and mathematics achievement in fourth grade is 0.35, and with Spanish achievement the correlation is 0.42, at the level of the individual child; the school-level correlation between percentage of children from non-Spanish origin in the school and the school's average achievement in Spanish is 0.57 (and our own research showed that such children are extremely slow at acquiring reading skills even in their own languages). In Chapter 2, it was shown in a multivariate context that having a language other than Spanish as a mother tongue, or coming from a non-Spanish-dominant environment (be it in the family or the community), is an important factor—identified by the Peruvian literature—in explaining low academic achievement. In Chapter 6, it was also shown that early literacy acquisition among Peruvian children is a serious problem: schools are taking three to four years, maybe five years, to do what in a proper school could be done in one or two years—suggesting a waste or inefficiency of some 30 percent at least, and perhaps as high as 60 percent in the early years of schooling.

Documentation of this problem is of course nothing new. Cummings and Tamayo (1994) refer to studies from the 1980s where this is already demonstrated. Multivariate analyses have also found that this effect tends to be (somewhat) independent of socioeconomic status or poverty; linguistic origin or the fact that a school is located in a bilingual region are, aside from poverty, barriers to achievement under current educational models. (It has to be noted, though, that these factors appear to be third in importance, after poverty and management factors.) In Chapter 4, we also saw that the learning performance of the poor is not only lower than that of the less poor, but that, more interestingly, it is less predictable. The variance in learning achievement among the poor is higher than the variance in learning achievement among the less poor. Poor and non-Spanish-origin individuals thus face a double burden; they receive a poorer education and are not even exactly sure what they are getting in the first place. At the same time, the fact that the education they receive is so variable—that in some schools the achievement among the poor is almost as high as among the rich—suggests that there are useful working models of pedagogy already available in Peru that require neither major discoveries nor technical adaptations. And this, in turn, implies that one of the issues confronting the education of those with non-Spanish origins is that of standards—from the availability of strong and accepted pedagogical models and teacher training in this area, to the actual *appropriate* standardization of the *teaching* vernacular language (which does not require a standardization of the generally spoken vernacular). Finally, we also saw in Chapter 1 that Peru, along with South Africa, is one of the countries with the highest internal educational inequality (of the 14 or so developing countries with good enough data, South Africa is the country with the most measured educational inequality in mathematics, Peru is second). All the facts discussed in this paragraph are related to each other in ways that do not require elaboration—they are not a set of coincidences. One final fact needs to be added: the evidence is clear, and has been for a long time, that children—including Peruvians—trained in *good* EIB programs do better in actually developing their Spanish abilities (see Cummins and Tamayo (1994)). As such, there are models—even within Peru—that seem to work and which have been known for quite some time.

The rest of this section summarizes what seems to be required in order to improve the learning performance of non-Spanish-origin segments of the population. It should be noted that the concern here is not the re-vitalization of non-Western languages. This is a related problem, but it is not the one that occupies us here. Our concern is with the educational and cognitive capital of the poor. The section then notes what Peru has done in this area thus far, and, by emphasizing the contrast between what is needed and what has been done, shows what remains to be done in Peru.

What Does it Take, and Is Peru Doing What it Takes?

There is some literature and there are guidelines on "what it takes" to properly implement EIB. The following matrix summarizes lessons learned in, for example, Dutcher (2004), Ndoye (2003), Tucker (1999), Danida (2004), D'Emilio (2002), and PREAL (2004). It adds more tentative lessons that emerge from an interpretation of this literature, rather than directly from the literature. Finally, the matrix shows to what degree the requirement has been properly addressed in Peru, based on our own review of: Trapnell and Neira (2004), Zúñiga, Sánchez and Zacharías (2000), Jung and López (1989), Vigil (2004), Guzmán, Penacho and Gonzáles (2002), Trapnell and others (2004), Rivero (2004), Oliart (2002), Red EBI Peru (1998), Kuper (1988), *Ministerio de Educación (2001)*, Grimaldo Vásquez (2003), Orr Easthhouse (2004), Zavala (2002), Trapnell and others (2004), and Cueto and Secada (2001), as well as key informant interviews.

Table 8.1. Tasks or Requirements Needed to Successfully Implement EIB and Degree of Presence in Peru	
Task or requirement needed to successfully implement EIB	**Degree of presence in Peru**
Development of mother tongue as a base for second language and other cognitive skills.	Recognized officially. However, relative to Bolivia, for example, the policy is weak, in that it does not sufficiently promote indigenous languages as important national languages, e.g., by calling for Spanish speakers to learn indigenous languages. See Hornberger (2000) and *Política de Educación Bilingüe Intercultural (1989)*. Other multicultural societies, such as South Africa, call for all youths to learn at least one other national language.[44]
Parental and community support.	Not sufficient, as programs currently implemented, though there is support from indigenous leadership. Degree of parental support would most likely increase if EIB was properly implemented and paid off as the research suggests it would, and if it was localized. The

(continued)

---

44. See http://www.polity.org.za/html/govdocs/policy/edulangpolicy.html?rebookmark=1, sourced on March 20, 2005. Interestingly, this aspect of the policy actually predates democratization. During *apartheid,* among whites, those of the Afrikaner (Dutch-origin) group were required to learn English, and those of the English group were required to learn Afrikaans, even though the media of instruction were separate and citizens had the choice of schools specializing in either medium of instruction. Typically, the better-off Afrikaners, traditionally the exploited group, learned English better than the well-off English learned Afrikaans. This relative "within-White" openness to multilingualism during the pre-democratic past may help in opening up the society to "White/non-White" multilingualism, though of course the cultural gap that must be bridged now is much greater.

Table 8.1. Tasks or Requirements Needed to Successfully Implement EIB and Degree of Presence in Peru (*Continued*)

Task or requirement needed to successfully implement EIB	Degree of presence in Peru
	poor quality alienates the parents. (E.g., children would learn Spanish better in a *proper* EIB program, and most likely parents would then be satisfied.) See Orr Easthouse (2004), López (2002), Uccelli (1999), Oliart (2002), and Zúñiga, Sánchez and Zacharías (2000). Furthermore, it is important to realize what "community support" might mean in a country such as Peru. Chapter 6 of this report shows how parents are often happy with the level of quality of education their children receive, even if it objectively seems poor. Nonetheless, parents do seem to have a concern over their children's acquisition of Spanish.
Teachers able to understand and use both languages, and prepared in bilingual instruction and inter-cultural competence.	Minimal, but public discourse on EIB is very aware of the need. Progress is being made, as teacher training institutions take on the need. However, up to date only nine teacher training colleges (out of several hundred) officially offer this specialty, and the first cohorts of graduates are only now exiting. Furthermore, four of these are in the Amazon region, which appears to be an imbalance. (See Oliart 2002, Trapnell and others 2004.) Teachers themselves often do not actually know how to *use* the language they are supposed to teach for writing. Worse, many of the trainers in EIB do not speak or use the languages (López 2002). Some apparently actually undermine EIB with parents (López 2002). One hopeful sign is the increased self-organization and interest of teachers as in, for example, national meetings on EIB which are not state-based. See López (2002).
"Localized standardization" of approaches *within* the indigenous languages, to include standardization of the language used for instruction, as well as discovery and diffusion of standard, effective pedagogical models.	Minimal, and public discourse does not seem cognizant of the need. Standardization is achieved in a bureaucratic manner and seems unrealistic because of lack of attention to local variants. Furthermore, standardization appears not to have been created, yet, with a proper degree of understanding of the complexities involved. In the opinion of some researchers, it appears as if the standardization proposed is similar to what would result in Europe if one were to standardize, say, Spanish and Italian around Latin, so as to economize on the production of books and materials in Spain and Italy. See Orr Easthouse (2004), Hornberger (2002), Zúñiga, Sánchez, and Zacharías (2002), Vigil (2004), Kuper (1988), Red EBI Peru (1999), and López (2002), who comments on lack of systems, standards, and indicators, and a big gap between theory and practice. The studies, taken together (with varying opinions among the authors) could be synthesized as recognizing the need for some standardization but with localized variants, in the case of language itself, and for standardization of pedagogical approaches based on solid research and local participation.

Table 8.1. Tasks or Requirements Needed to Successfully Implement EIB and Degree of Presence in Peru (*Continued*)	
Task or requirement needed to successfully implement EIB	**Degree of presence in Peru**
Thorough national research and evaluation processes that allow "cycles of discovery" rather than importation of models or dependence on a "once-and-for all" approach.	Weak, not just in EIB, but in education in general. Though there is a very good education research industry in Peru in general, there is weak linkage between research and policymaking and policy-enforcement, and, specifically, EIB-oriented research is incipient. There are some examples of an incipient cycle of discovery (research and feedback) such as in PEEB-Puno and FORMABIAP. But in general the opinion of key informants and the literature is that there is very little evaluation-based learning going on. See Zúñiga, Sánchez, and Zacharías (2000), Jung and López (1989), and Trapnell and Neira (2004). There is little evaluation of results against any reading and literacy targets (Trapnell and others 2004). Considering the large number of EIB projects that has been funded (see Table 8.2), this is a considerable waste. Had there been a serious interest in a cycle of evaluation and learning, there would now be powerful lessons, instead of widely dispersed opinions, and there could be strong national programs.
Proper planning and resourcing commensurate with the task, availability of materials teachers would actually want to use.	Weak. Education spending in Peru is low, in general, and human resourcing is weak (great instability in positions). EIB is also poorly resourced, and seems to be resourced too much at the insistence of donors, and with donor funding. A common complaint among key informants and in much of the literature is that most of the support seems to come from international organizations. See López (2022), and Trapnell and Neira (2004).
A decentralized system characterized by "decentralization with standards" that can provide the space for diversity while respecting need for accountability.	Incipient, though actors are keenly aware of the opportunity decentralization represents and are beginning to take advantage of this. However, there seems to be very little clarity about how one achieves "decentralization with standards", how one can have standards with diversity, etc., though there is some increasing awareness of this (see Trapnell and Neira (2004) on the notion of procedural rights to produce localized norms). EIB itself is still a centralized program. Key informants were of the opinion that indigenous groups are consulted and do give opinions (which is progress) but are not involved in crafting solutions in a decentralized manner.

Sources: Elaborated by the authors from the reports cited and key informants as noted.

The results of the table should be fairly convincing that efforts towards improved EIB in Peru are insufficient. The table also points out the directions in which more effort is needed. It also highlights, by reference to key studies such as Jung and López (1989) and Kuper (1988) that date back at least 15 years, the fact that much of this is not new. Furthermore, even if the many existing projects (see Table 8.2) have not been formally evaluated, it would seem that much of what has been learned should be codifiable into useful standards, even in an *ex-post* manner, if sufficient effort and leadership were to be devoted to this issue. The fact that after so many projects there is still so much fundamental uncertainty and hesitation in Peru about "what to do" and "how to do it" betokens a basic lack of political will to do something truly meaningful, or perhaps to admit that what has been done is not what the indigenous themselves want. In other words, if the knowledge of what is needed is old, a logical conclusion is that what is lacking is political will and leadership to carry out a properly honest synthesis of studies, dialogue and "concertación," and the determination of a rational and consensus-based policy that can then be funded and properly implemented (Trapnell and others 2004, Rivero 2004). Insufficient leadership at the Ministry of Education and in regional authorities is clearly part of the cause. Furthermore, many of the points in Table 8.1 are officially recognized by at least some officials (Ministerio de Educación 2001). This is, in other words, a serious failure of "compact." One key area is worth

Table 8.2. Projects in Educación Intercultural Bilingüe in Peru

Project	Institution	Timing	Place
Program for Experimental Education for Quechua-speaking children	Plan for Linguistic Development, then Center for Applied Linguistics (CILA) of San Marcos University	1966–1984	Quinua, Ayacucho
Project for Experimental Bilingual Education in Puno (PEEB-P)	German Development Cooperation (GTZ) and Ministry of Education	1977–1991	Puno: Quechua and Aymara communities
Program for Rural Andean School (ERA)	Radda Barnen Stockholm (Save the Children) and Ministry of Education	1988–1995	Cusco and Puno
Program for Bilingual Intercultural Education of the High Napo (PEBIAN)	Missionaries in the Angosteros community	1975	Napo Kichwa and a Secoya community
Education project with the Candoshi	Terra Nova	1980	Chuinda, Chapuri, and Huitoyacu rivers
Project for Bilingual Intercultural Education for the Ashaninka	Amazonian Center for Anthropology and Practical Applications (CAAP)	1983–1987	Tambo river
Training of Bilingual Teachers for the Peruvian Amazon (FORMABIAP)	Loreto Teacher Training Institute AIDESEP	1988–2004	Central and Northeast Amazon
Project in Bilingual Intercultural Education in Andahuaylas Chincheros (PEBIACH)	Anton Spinoy Foundation	1990–2002	Andahuaylas and Chincheros
National Teacher Training Program—Bilingual Intercultural Education (PLANCAD—EBI)	Ministry of Education and executing agencies under contract	1996–2004	Seven departments or regions
Education Project for Rural Areas (PEAR)	Ministry of Education	2002–2004	Canas, in Cusco, Frías and Suyo in Piura and El Dorado in San Martín

Source: Compiled for this report by the authors.

discussing at greater length than the table allows, because it is central to the arguments in the rest of this report. This is the issue of standards. There are many reasons why EIB is not working as well as it could in Peru. However, from the literature reviewed, and as suggested by the table above, these appear to be relatively well understood. The issue of standards, on the other hand, seems to be clouded by confusion and controversy.

A Special Issue Related to "Compact" and Accountability: Standards and Standardization in EIB[45]

Analysis of EIB experience in Bolivia suggests that Bolivia has made more recent progress with EIB than Peru has (D'Emilio 1996). There may be many reasons for this. An important one may be that the PEIB project in Bolivia—unlike others of its kind that developed different alphabets and educational materials for different varieties of each language—emphasized linguistic standardization and consolidation of the 'larger identities,' which has created new ties of solidarity in areas where excessive development of local terms had sharpened differences. Under the motto "one language must unite and not divide the group that speaks it," a single alphabet has been used for all varieties of each language. This "has allowed for a degree of linguistic development and consolidation that is unprecedented in Bolivian history" (D'Emilio 1996). Not only were languages standardized, but this was accomplished as a common effort not imposed by the government.

However, in the opinion of some authors, the approach to standardization undertaken by the Peruvian government has been naïve at best, and may, at worst, actually undermine learning in the indigenous language (Orr Easthouse 2004; Vigil 2004). This may be the result of a situation where standardization has been imposed on language variants as different from each other, in the opinion of some linguists, as Spanish is from Portuguese or from Italian. (This applies to Quechua variants in particular—variants which are, within Peru, quite different from each other.) Creating a standardized variant of, say, Spanish and Italian would require reaching so far back to the original Latin roots that the standardized variant would itself be largely unrecognizable by either the Spanish or Italian speakers (Orr Easthouse 2004).[46] Many authors recognize the need for standardization, while others call for attention to local variants, and yet others call for both simultaneously (Hornberger 2002; Zúñiga, Sánchez, and Zacharías 2002; Vigil 2004; Kuper 1988; Red EBI Peru 1999; López 2002).

It is clear that there are advantages to standardization. They include most obviously the achievement of economies of scale in, for example, materials production. Most importantly (and most germane to the accountability approach taken in this report), however, without standards there can be no accountability, or at least no bureaucratic accountability. More accurately, if there are no standards, public accountability becomes so costly—so mired in constant transacting—that it is difficult to achieve in any but the wealthiest or most culturally homogeneous societies. In order for standards to lower transaction costs

---

45. In this section "standards" can refer to standards of learning, to the use of a locally-standardized teaching language, or to proven and effective standard pedagogical models.

46. Why a country, or even a group of countries, would attempt to standardize something so difficult to standardize is unknown. Various authors cite political reasons (such as the need to create a unified voting bloc), technical naiveté in linguistics, excessive faith in what could be achieved through economies of scale, the fact that even EIB itself is assimilationist, and other factors (Orr Easthouse 2004, Hornberger 2000).

and result in affordable systems of accountability, they have to be partially "artificial" by definition, and this is true of any standard. This is the paradox. If public funding is being used, and particularly if this public funding is central (for example, via fiscal transfers), rather than own-source localized public funding, then imposing a form of accountability that must be somewhat bureaucratic and to some degree "artificial" is simply inevitable. For the foreseeable future, the funding of education in Peru, including funding for bilingual education will continue to be based on fiscal transfers given that relying on own-source local tax revenues is not only impractical but highly inequitable. Hence, there is likely to be a need for continued bureaucratic accountability, which requires the existence of some form of standards. In an accountable system, if there are central fiscal transfers, there is a need to account for the productivity of the funding used across units of subnational government, and this requires the existence of standards. It must ultimately be possible to tell which sub-national units are doing better than others, and within subnational units, which areas or schools are doing better than others. This is key not just to accountability but to the targeting of interventions and assistance.

However, to use a commercial analogy, if economies of scale, through the use of standards, are achieved in the production of a good for which there is then no consumer demand (because the good has become "bland" and appeals to no specific consumers), then the standardization is not only useless but counterproductive. Similarly, if a standards agency imposes weights and measures on a market to promote accountability of producers to consumers and to lower the transaction costs involved in this accountability, but this is done in such a way that the goods traded are thereby devalued by the consumers themselves, then, again, the standardization is worse than useless. In Peru's language approach this appears to be a distinct possibility (Orr Easthouse 2004). But there may be ways to deal with the apparent contradiction or paradox between the need for standards and the need for localized adaptation (some of which are suggested in, for example, Hornsberger (2004), but require much attention to detail and clear thinking). Clarity on how this could be done, in a decentralizing context, has not yet arisen among the intellectual leadership of Peru, though ideas are emerging (such as the call for localized procedural rights to the creation of norms and standards as in Trapnell and Neira (2004)). This would be a fruitful area for technical assistance and policy dialogue. As discussions among linguists show (del Rosario and Warren 2003; Luykx 2004; Hornberger and Coronel-Molina 2004; Orr Easthouse 2004), resolving this problem is not a simple matter. Furthermore, inevitably, some compromises and tradeoffs will exist (as total local adaptation is impossible, if standards are indeed to be maintained and excessive costs are to be avoided). It should be noted that a localized approach to standardization, while expensive, does avoid the high transaction costs involved in creating very broad consensus. Creating broader standards, even if linguistically possible, would require crafting broad consensus, which would be very costly (in time if not in fiscal resources) and could lead to paralysis or very slow progress. To some extent, this is what has been happening in Peru with the issue of standards. Thus, the economies achievable through broad standards may be somewhat illusory. That standards are possible in language instruction for relatively small groups is exemplified by the development of standards of teaching in foreign languages in the United States, where standards have been, to a reasonable degree, successfully promoted by the American Council of the Teaching of Foreign Languages (ACTFL undated). Similarly, individual states in the United States, facing significant immigration of children of Spanish-speaking origin, have managed to develop very clear and detailed standards that use proper sequencing between grades for the teaching of English as a second language (Public Schools of North Carolina 2003). Other states have created bilingual programs, and these also have standards. The task is by no means impossible, though it requires resources and attention to detail.

Decentralization makes new options available. In a decentralized country, approaches that assess and reward the willingness of sub-national communities to value their own learning variants can be tried. Matching grants systems that can underwrite the development of localized standards would be one approach. (Central work to sort out equivalences would still be needed.) Relatively expensive localized standard-setting (such as in the case of languages spoken by relatively small numbers of persons, such as variants of Quechua) can thus be supported by a central government, but only if the sub-national community is willing to make own-source efforts to co-pay for the system. The own-source efforts need not literally rely on local taxation as this may be inequitable and impractical; they may simply require the willingness to allocate parts of a block transfer to the language issue, to match an earmarked grant (it would thus require both a block grant and a targeted grant system). In this manner the central government provides support for equity reasons but does so by using the community's willingness-to-pay (by diverting some of its block grant) as an indicator of seriousness and organization on the part of the recipients. The matching ratio can be generous, as a way to mitigate poverty and inequality problems. If "the community" of speakers is not geographically localized to be coterminous with political governance districts, the matching grants systems can encourage dispersed communities of speakers of a similar variant to coalesce "from the ground up" even if they are not neighbors. This can then achieve some economies of scale. The funding system would act as an inducement carrot rather than as a bureaucratic stick, and would decentralize and "communitize" the transaction costs involved in coming to agreement. Furthermore, it removes the politics involved from the national stage. The optimal size of "the local" would then tend to be organically determined as an equilibrium between the economics of the grants system and the dissimilarities between the variants of the languages, rather than being bureaucratically imposed. Furthermore, with a proper grants system, groups would hire their own linguists, researchers and facilitators to assist them, again putting the communities of speakers in charge.

It is also necessary to admit that the linguistic complexity of Peru may be such that the "community of interests" may not really overlap with political decentralization. If there are essentially infinite gradients in language mixes and needs, and these interact in complex ways, the language policy needs to take advantage not of decentralization but, at the extreme, of school autonomy. In this case, a fiscal grants system related to decentralization that is used to create standards may help, but much more is needed. Additionally, it may be necessary to allow schools to choose (some of) the standards to which they are willing to be held accountable and offer them options for learning how to deliver against those standards.

Finally, it should be noted that the possible policy suggestion emerging above is not to recommend a "free-for-all" system of grants. Some central body would need to establish criteria and methods for providing such grants, and all this would have to take place within the context of a global policy on EIB that sets out the overall objectives as a national policy. Furthermore, the context would also have to exist to create effective models of "pedagogical delivery to standard." It is not sufficient to create standards. A context that can rigorously evaluate effective pedagogical models for delivery to standard does not yet exist.

The resources needed to attract intellectual capacity to this task, and the technical capacity itself, have not yet been devoted to the task, as noted in Table 8.1.

In conclusion, there are options to move the situation forward. The options for dealing with some of the more obvious issues, such as teacher training for EIB, are already covered in the literature cited. Thus, it is clear in the case of the more obvious options that if things do not progress it is for lack of political will or implementation skill, not for lack of technical policy options. This section has noted that there are thornier technical problems, for example those related to standards. But there are options for dealing with these difficult issues, and some have been suggested. The options in question have not yet been fully explored in the Peruvian literature, which is why this section has gone to some length to illustrate what such options might consist of. Further discussion of and policy dialogue around these sorts of options would most likely be of benefit to the EIB sector in Peru.

CHAPTER 9

Participation and Decentralization

Little Effect, Some Potential[47]

O ther chapters have dealt indirectly with the issue of accountability to parents. In Chapter 6, it was noted that the fact that most parents are in fact happy with the quality of schooling at their schools—when objective evidence suggests the quality of schooling is very poor—is worrisome in that it creates an accountability problem. If parents are basically happy, it seems unlikely that, in the absence of certain improvements in parental overview of schools, parental pressure could be relied on to improve quality. On the other hand, it was noted in Chapter 7, where effective public schools and the *FyA* models were discussed, that the best schools are indeed those that are focused on delivering to parents and community (though not necessarily those where parents are heavily involved in school governance). This chapter looks at the issues of participation at the local level, as well as voice at the regional or national level, as instruments of accountability.

The main conclusions of the chapter are that while in Peru there is a great deal of *potential* participation and voice given the existence, in a formal sense, of many "spaces" and opportunities for the expression of voice, in reality there is little *effective* voice in the education sector for parents and ordinary citizens (including the private sector and the poor). The main reasons for this appear to be:

a) unsolved classical collective action problems, namely that it is not in the interest of specific parents to militate to solve the problems of all children,

b) lack of standards and a perception of rights specifically around quality issues, which makes it difficult for citizens to know when their rights or entitlements are being

---

47. This chapter was prepared partially on the basis of input from Flavio Figallo in a consultant's report prepared entitled "De Altavoces y Audífonos en la Educación."

violated and hence prevents organization and the expression of grievance; in short, a lack of effective demand for quality,

c) the fact that most voice mechanisms are captured by the providers,

d) weak legislation (contradictory, overlapping, complex, and unclear duties and powers) regulating the bodies implementing voice, and, finally,

e) lack of effective power to go along with voice and participation.

The following paragraphs document these issues in some detail, first at the most local level, namely the school, and then at higher levels. It is noted that while the current situation is not very positive, there are some positive trends, and some suggestions are made for how to accentuate the positive potential for voice and participation.

School Level

In our survey of schools, we noted that some 89 percent of parents are happy with the quality of education their children receive. This echoes the findings of the National Evaluation, where a similar percentage of "happiness" is found. This level of happiness appears not to be due to a basic lack of information, as we discovered in our survey. We surveyed a good mix of APAFA members and non-members. In general, the following findings corroborate the fact that parents are in fact informed (in the literal sense of being provided with information). First, 93 percent of parents state that the principal of the school has meetings with them to keep them informed of school matters. The plurality (though not the majority) of those giving answers (40 percent) stated that the main theme of discussion is, in fact, student achievement. A good bit of information is also provided regarding the school's work plan (25 percent of parents mentioning this aspect). The percentages of parents reporting that teachers keep them informed was even higher: 96 percent. And the percentage of parents saying that the information conveyed related to children's achievement was even higher than the percentage for the same attributed to principals (78 percent). All of this hardly suggests a situation where parents are kept in the dark regarding quality matters through the sheer non-provision of information. The failure is elsewhere: either in a basic lack of demand for quality, or in a lack of demand generated by the fact that there is no articulation of rights to quality, or normed expectations, for parents to form their ideas about quality (such as that a child should be able to read fluently by the end of grade 2, along with examples and data on which children in fact do).

When asked what they wished the APAFA would do more of, most parents (63 percent) mentioned that it should provide more infrastructure; only one parent mentioned that the APAFA should take more interest in learning achievement. Again, this suggests a situation where most parents identify "good education" with mere access to facilities, and have little sense of education as having to do with cognitive development.

The picture that emerges is one where information is in fact provided, but where there is either no normed basis for providing information about achievement, or no inherent demand for it. When asked whether there were prescribed formats for the provision of information (of any kind) to parents, 86 percent of school directors responded "no." Thus, though by regulation APAFAs and parents have a right to information, and this right is actually implemented, the information supplied appears to be ineffective and lacking in reference to any norm (either a norm regarding the type of information to be provided, or the fact that information needs to be provided against some norm of achievement). Only about 50 percent of parents claimed to be aware of what their rights as parents were (and even this seems high, given our main hypothesis), but only 50 percent of those (25 percent of the total) could describe how they got a sense of those rights. Unfortunately we did not ask for their opinion of what those rights were, so it is difficult to know whether "yes, I know I have rights" was a conditioned social response or represents a real awareness of educational rights or entitlements based on some norms or expectations, such as the right to have one's child be able to read by a certain age.

The positive aspect in all this is that information transactions do in fact happen. In this sense, if there was a more common basis of information on rights to cognitive achievement, built around some standards of learning, perhaps more progress could be made. However, it is also apparent that most parents probably would have to be educated about these rights, and that this would take considerable time. The inherent demand for quality appears low. Thus, the belief that a faster move towards parental power and school autonomy could—in the absence of much stronger standards and parental education—lead to increases in school quality, would seem quite unjustified.

Levels Above the School

At levels above the school there is a veritable florescence of "spaces" for educational participation. If the creation of committees, forums, councils, and so forth could by itself lead to improved education and effective representation of those affected by poor education (citizens as parents, and the users of labor in business), Peru's educational future would be assured. The following is a more or less complete list of bodies with a specific educational role. There are also bodies with a general social or poverty-fighting role, such as the *Mesas de Concertación de Lucha Contra la Pobreza;* these are not analyzed here to keep things simple:

- A national association of APAFAs, the CENAPAFA. (In fact, there are two, the CENAPAFA, and a splinter from it, the FENAPAFA.)
- *Consejo Nacional de Educación.*
- *Foro Educativo.*
- The legislature's *Comisión de Educación, Cultural, Ciencia y Tecnología.*
- At provincial level, the *Consejo Participativo Local de Educación* (COPALES), associated with the UGEL.
- At regional level, the *Consejo Participativo Regional de Educación* (COPARES), associated with the DRE.
- At school level, the *Asociación de Padres de Familia* (APAFA) and the *Consejo Educativo Institucional* (CEI).
- In addition to these "bodies" there have been processes of national consultation around education policy. Some of these processes bleed into and merge with each other, so it is a little difficult to state how many there have been, but over the past decade or so there appear to have been three or four distinct, fairly large-scale and reasonably well-organized formal consultative processes on education policy.

As noted, in theory, if these bodies and processes worked well, the citizens' voice would be well-represented and heard. However, these bodies do not work as well as one would hope. The following are the main problems, illustrated via reference to particular bodies and processes.

Many of these bodies are simply captured by special interests. The CENAPAFA and the *Comisión* of the legislature, for example, could be said to be largely captured by teachers, and to speak for and represent teachers, not citizens. Furthermore, their creation appears to have been fostered by political parties or movements, not spontaneously by citizens or as a result of multi-partisan legislative efforts. *Foro Educativo* is composed of prominent citizens, but most of them are professional educators in some sense (for example, former Ministers or high-level executive branch officials) and are part of the provider establishment. The CENAPAFA, supposedly a parents' organization, rarely takes positions that differ from that of the SUTEP, the teacher's union, and is headed by a former teacher who happens to be a member of the union. The legislature's *Comisión* is largely populated by ex-teachers (a large plurality, though not a majority), and most of its legislative work has to do with either the creation of jobs for teachers, or improvements in working conditions for teachers. The reason why this capture takes place has to do with classical problems of collective action and information. First, parents are poorly (though actively, as noted above) informed. Moreover, it is not really rational for most parents to make monetary contributions and be activists at levels higher than the school: a classic free-rider problem. The free-rider problem is compounded by the fact that public schools are quite heterogeneous. Thus, the free-rider effect is created not only by the usual problem of dispersed costs and the feeling that if one does not take action someone else will, but by the fact that the actors confronting these feelings range from the very poor and rural to the relatively well-off and urban. This makes it difficult to generate the financial contributions needed to defend a common view, which leaves a vacuum. This space is therefore "captured" by those whose interests are very concentrated: the teachers. In short, in Peru, as in most poor countries, it seems unlikely that one can rely on aggregated voice—which arises spontaneously from citizens—to put pressure on the executive branch or the service providers. The executive branch of government exists to solve problems of collective action, but is easily captured by the interests of the providers themselves; the same thing happens to bodies that could otherwise serve as watchdogs over the executive branch. They too suffer from a collective action problem. The shortcuts to accountability through citizen pressure groups that societies could use when legislatures are not representative, and when policymakers do not respond to the needs of citizens, appear to be somewhat blocked, at least for now.

The *Consejo Nacional de Educación* is a statutory body appointed by the Minister of Education. Thus, from a structural perspective, it seems difficult that it would serve a critical or watchdog function, and indeed it mostly does not, given that it appears to have few opinions that are critical of the executive branch, and acts more as a group that produces technical opinions and support for the executive branch. Furthermore, 40 percent of the leadership of the CNE overlaps with the *Foro Educativo*, which, as mentioned, is composed largely of providers. Thus, again, the CNE appears to largely represent providers. The few non-provider citizens, for example, representatives of the private sector, appear relatively non-active and, as noted, are very few in number. Its technical secretariat (as opposed to the *Consejo* per se), however, does appear to possess quite a bit of independence from the traditional provider establishment, judging by the professional background of the technicians.

Both *Foro Educativo* and the CNE also appear at times to be collections of individual consultants and thinkers who are engaged in producing policy studies or positions for the government or donors. They also seem to implement delivery or consultation projects, sometimes using donor funding. Thus, at least part of their function appears to be more characteristic of implementation and consulting NGOs, rather than of true advocacy and research think-tanks. This no doubt has to do with their sources of funding.

There are new organizations related to the process of decentralization, namely the COPAREs and the COPALEs. These are regional or provincial bodies that play a "legislative" or "representative" role at regional and local level, as the counterparts of the DRE and the UGEL. The legislation creating these institutions is very recent, and the specific norming is still in draft form. Many of these institutions are either not functioning yet, or are only incipiently functioning. Unfortunately, the norming framework is sometimes ambiguous: many of the attributions are overlapping, contradictory, incomplete, or subservient to the sub-national executive branch (the DRE or the UGEL). The representativity of these bodies is, under current norming, corporativist rather than truly representative or democratic, and is thus inherently likely to suffer from capture.

In addition to "bodies" there have been large-scale consultative processes, often led by the bodies. In 1997, *Foro Educativo* promoted an *Acuerdo Nacional* in opposition to the Fujimori-era policies of the Ministry of Education. In 2001, the then Minister initiated a large scale consultative process to set the tone for education policy in the post-Fujimori era. This process was truly large scale, very well-organized, and resulted in large volumes of well-presented information. In 2002 another consultative process was launched to legitimize and to some degree shape the new education law that eventually emerged in 2003. Finally, in 2004 and 2005 there was a process that led to the "Pacto Social de Compromisos Recíprocos" and the *Proyecto Educativo Nacional.* Many of the current members of the CNE took leadership positions in these consultative processes. Furthermore, these consultative processes do create some consistent sets of results and recommendations. This is due in part to the fact that many of the actors who generally participate in efforts of this kind participate in process after process. Because of their very nature and broad base and appeal, however, the recommendations tend to be well-meaning wish lists; the difficult and more controversial issues are often avoided and "left for later."

A Way Forward on Voice and Participation? Opportunities and Dangers in Decentralization

A possible but insufficient source of hope is that all of these institutions are new, and therefore represent a positive trend. However, this is not exactly the case. The basic shape of most of the institutions is quite old, but they have had to undergo various legal changes over time. Some version of APAFA has existed in law and in practice since 1941, but the CENAPAFA itself is a much more recent creation, and one apparently sponsored to a significant degree by political-partisan interests. *Foro Educativo* was created in 1992. The CNE has antecedents that go back as far as 1959, though the specific legislation first appears only in 1982. It is mentioned again in legislation in 1992, but it was not until 2002 when, under a decree rather than a law, it came fully into being. CNE is supposed to have its own law, but so far it does not. While these institutions have been around for a long time, however, it is also true that their more recent evolution gives them more "teeth" and more capacity to extract accountability. For example, it is only recently that APAFAs were empowered to demand accountability for learning results. Thus, the movement is at least going in the right general direction.

The process of decentralization is also a cause for optimism. Without a doubt, the more progressive regions will move ahead of others, creating laboratories of accountability and representativity that can be models for other regions or provinces. In fact, some regions are moving ahead of the national government and are creating regional education plans (*Proyecto Educativo Regional*) even though the national education plan (*Proyecto Educativo Nacional*) is not finished and norms for crafting the *Proyecto Educativo Regional* have never been made clear.

Another source of hope is that these institutions do at least provide some accountability for continuity, and an institutional "home" for some continuity of policy. One of the major policy problems confronted by Peru is the extreme instability in education policy created by the fact that Ministers have changed about every eight months in the last few decades. Many institutions such as *Foro Educativo* and the CNE are populated by ex-Ministers and ex-officials under various Ministries. Given their prestige and power of convocation, these institutions are in fact able to demand some accountability for the continuation of major policies, and create some continuity in thinking around major policy issues. However, in order to finish the agenda, Peru could consider several policy options.

First, accountability, and its basis in participation and voice, should start at the lowest level possible. Peru's most recent legislation, the *Ley General de Educación,* creates the legal space for giving the *Consejo Educativo Institucional* more power. The CEIs could be normed to represent parents by giving parents a statutory majority. Parents' capacity to demand accountability could be increased if schools received direct per capita funding and CEIs had to approve the budget that plans the use of these funds. More power could be given to parents if numerical, standard expectations of learning were developed and popularized so that they could begin to see these levels of learning as rights, and if standard measurement and reporting formats were created. Finally, CEIs could play a sharper role in teacher evaluation and selection, again on the basis of standards of performance (which would have to be created first).

Second, the legislation and norming around local and regional participatory bodies should be clearer and simpler. The powers and duties of these bodies should be made less contradictory and overlapping with those of other bodies, unlike the current situation where everyone is seemingly involved or in charge of the same task. Furthermore, these bodies should be made less dependent on the regional or local executive branch and the national executive (the DRE and the UGEL), and could be given more real powers (for example, power to approve certain budgets).

Third, some of the national voice mechanisms should receive more solid, permanent funding that is more independent of particular Ministers. To prevent the posts funded in this manner from becoming semi-academic sinecures, and therefore to prevent institutions from lapsing into irrelevance, selection for the boards and executive directorships of the institutions should be competitive and term-limited. Performance indicators for the institutions, based on the production of policy-relevant feedback and watchdog functions, could be created. All efforts to make representation in these bodies corporativist (one representative from the union, one from the parents, and so forth) should be resisted.

Educational decentralization in Peru has started; a basic legislative and normative framework is either in place or is taking shape. As of the writing of this document, however, the state of decentralization in practice (and even in regulation) is fluid and confused to such an extent that it is impossible to make forecasts as to whether decentralization is likely to make all of the problems listed here worse or better. There are various options for using decentralization to improve quality, but several dangers also exist. Neither the dangers nor the opportunities are real yet. Maximizing the potential is likely to require significant work in crafting a regime of accountability at the regional level. The work required is discussed below.

On the positive side, decentralization could have a beneficial impact if the regional leaderships (the regional president, the "gerente social", and the head of the DRE) are forced to take responsibility for the quality of education in their jurisdictions, are required to compete with each other (or at least compare themselves to each other), and are given the authority to address problems. This would require that, for example, comparative information on school performance be available on a region by region basis (since presumably most of the authority will be at that level and at school level) and disseminated to citizens and regional representative bodies (both general, namely the *Consejo Regional* and *Consejo de Coordinación Regional,* for example, and specific, namely the *Consejo Participativo Regional de Educación*) in order for these two groups to hold the local executives (such as the DRE) accountable for school performance. This information can also be used by the national government (or civil society) to enhance the accountability of regional authorities to their local citizenry by publishing comparative data. However, the regional authorities would have to have full ability to respond to problems that show up in comparative performance data; for example, they would have to be able to move personnel around, allocate resources to particular problems, and be able to innovate. In this sense, decentralization could take advantage of the fact that some regional leaders are likely to be more innovative and interested in education than others. With decentralization, the country will have a larger variety of approaches to tackling problems; regions can experiment with a variety of practices, and the likelihood that best practices will emerge is enhanced. But for the country as a whole to benefit from this variety of practices, a centralized process for studying good practice, and spreading it, is needed. Few (if any) countries in Latin America have been able to craft these kinds of systems in order to benefit from decentralization. It is far from clear that, as it is shaping up, decentralization in Peru is going in the direction needed for quality improvement.

There are also various dangers. A clear one is confusion. Current legislation in Peru is creating such a variety of participatory and parliament-like bodies, and with such vague language, that confusion over roles and conflict over jurisdictions is all but inevitable. (And, in many cases, in practice, one jurisdiction is given control over a neighboring one, if one of them is considered weak, instead of control reverting to the higher-level government. Thus, some "stronger" UGELs have executive authority over other, "weaker" UGELs, instead of control of the weaker UGELs reverting to the DRE. This is a recipe for chaos and conflict, and indeed this is what one finds, repeatedly, throughout Peru.) At the same time, executive branch bodies (such as the DRE and the UGEL) have both horizontal (to their own regional government) and vertical (to national Ministries, in particular education and finance) accountability lines that overlap and are not at all clear. This can and does lead to confusion and evasion of responsibilities. Finally, though (most of) education, as a sectoral competence, is allocated to regions, the reality is that a region is so large that, in terms of the accountability triangle discussed above, the citizens are not sufficiently closer to the top of the pyramid to make the voice mechanism much more powerful than if the top of the pyramid is simply the national government. Nor are the policymakers and the regional level close enough to the delivery points (schools) to make the norms stronger or truly more sensitive to local conditions, or to make problem detection at the school level any easier. In short, whether a school is one of fifteen hundred (in a region) or one of forty thousand (in the country) will probably not make much practical difference to accountability, even if it does make some difference to local adaptation and client preference.

In these regards, it is some form of school autonomy (contemplated in the current education law, but largely unimplemented) oriented at autonomy of management prerogatives such as control over teachers, but with centralized standards and testing, that might ultimately bring the service close enough to the citizens to make a significant difference to learning achievement. Most of the recommendations in the rest of this report are oriented to enhancing this sort of localized accountability.

CHAPTER 10

Policy Recommendations

This chapter summarizes the main sector-wide policy recommendations arising from the analysis in all the previous chapters and which address the key policy issues: quality and its distribution. Some of the chapters, such as Chapter 5, on dropout behavior, and Chapter 8, on bilingual education, have some specific recommendations that are not reproduced here.

Standards

Standards are needed in three key areas: learning (outcome standards), service to communities and to schools ("process" standards), and resource allocation. Without standards, accountability is either impossible or consumes too much social energy in transaction costs; standards are the currency, or the weights and measures, of accountability and help to economize on the informational content of transaction costs. Similarly, it is only the application of standards that gives meaning to the notion of a right to education once mass-scale enrollment exists. Thus, standards are the key not only to efficiency, but also to a rights-oriented approach to quality and equity of quality. "Standards" refers generically to three sets of things: (a) standardized, simplified, and transparent ways of doing things in a manner that reduces discretion and transaction costs, such as allocating resources via formulas based on enrollment (or attendance) and poverty; (b) setting metrics of performance—such as performance on reading as measured by a test or service standards for UGELs to provide services to schools—that do not set actual goals for a level on that test; and finally (c) actually setting goals, such as reaching a certain level on a reading test.

Peru needs much clearer learning standards, especially in the early grades, and needs to focus particularly on reading achievement. These standards need to be developed and disseminated. The current approach is too vague. The need for local and regional adaptation is, currently, being used as an excuse for mediocrity. It is possible to develop standards that are locally adapted yet that provide both ambition and a metric for accountability. The ambition to simultaneously develop standards for the whole system should be resisted. Peru needs to start with *reading* (and perhaps writing) standards, and with the *early grades*. Standards should be simple, should emphasize skill, and should be meaningful particularly to teachers and parents. With regard to reading, Peru should at first develop a simple and universal metric applied to every child in every school (and publicize school-level achievement against this metric), with a goal in mind of reaching a certain value on that metric (for example, 60 words read correctly per minute by the end of grade 2) within five years. Standards could focus on comprehension as a goal, and on speed (or fluency) of reading as an important measured instrument. Standards should be grade specific, or perhaps even specific to semesters within the school year. The simpler standards in the earlier grades could be developed first, and the rest of the system, meaning the later grades, could be tackled later. The idea is not to fixate the system on literacy in the early grades, but to *start* there both chronologically and in terms of priority as the basis for all other later skills. If the standards set for the lower grades cannot be set and met, the prognosis for the more advanced grades will not be good.

Standards need to allow for cultural and regional diversity, and yet remain standards. This can be done in a variety of ways to which Peru has not yet devoted sufficient attention. Matching-grant systems that require local effort, for example, could be developed as a way to stimulate standards that are applicable to particular regions, or adaptation of standards to intercultural and bilingual education (EIB).

One possible focus on learning standards that Peru could consider is a secondary-school exit exam. It would be possible to generate this process gradually and with less conflict by, for example, creating nationwide prizes for those who pass an exam that would initially be voluntary (only those aiming for the prize would take the exam, though one may wish to do it for whole schools rather than individuals, for reasons discussed below). Should this process find social acceptability, and as it leads to a refinement of the exit exam, the exit exam could be made mandatory. This kind of exit exam tends to drive parental and student pressure for school accountability, and this accountability pressure in turn tends to trickle down to primary schools (as feeder schools), though this takes a long time. It would be possible to create prize systems that are sensitive to differential starting conditions, by, for example giving prizes at the school level (for example, if a whole school volunteers for the system), by giving awards to the top marks-earners at any given school, by recognizing progress rather than actual achievement, or using statistical controls that create peer groups (as in Chile's National Teacher Performance Evaluation System [SNED]).

Service or process standards should be developed over time via observation of successful practice under difficult or average conditions. Schools that outperform others under similar conditions could be studied, and the good practices they engage in should eventually find their way into the procedural norms and standards. Current practice in Peru is for these procedural norms to be based on vague theories and bureaucratic needs, rather than on school-level practice and need. The next wave of Peruvian education research should focus on this issue.

Standards for teacher selection, embodied in exams that would have to be passed before individuals can become teachers, should also be created. These should be coordinated with standards for pre-service teacher training. Peru is currently considering these issues in the drafting of the new law on *Carrera Pública Magisterial* and in debates on accreditation of teacher training institutions. A new career ladder that promises better pay for better teachers will also help retain and attract better teachers.

Better funding standards are also needed, particularly as the country decentralizes and increases school-level autonomy under new legislation. This should take the form of a formula-based transfer of funds and physical resources from the national level to regions and from regions to schools. Formulas will lower transaction costs and will increase transparency and trust. They will also make it possible to target spending where it is needed most, in terms of both equity and results orientation. Finally, these formulas enable a sense of rights, in that schools and parents can have a clearer sense of the minimum funding to which they are entitled. A minimum per-student funding could be created, such as funding a basic minimum package of items including stationery, classroom supplies, cleaning materials, and so forth. The package could be more generous in poorer regions.

Finally, the UGELs, or the administrative unit above the school, should set standards of service to schools, and schools should set standards of service to parents and communities. Parents and communities should rate schools, and schools should rate UGELs. Comparative data should be publicized. After a few years, goals on these standards should be defined.

Accountability

While standards are needed for accountability, because otherwise there is no metric to which to hold anyone accountable, it is also true that without accountability pressure, standards do not do much good. Coming up to standard requires effort; effort should be rewarded and lack of effort should be punished. Thus, incentives are needed to drive accountability. To increase accountability pressure, the following steps are needed.

- Measure results at all schools in key areas of knowledge, not just in a sample of schools, concentrating first on reading in the early grades. Start publishing data on learning results and on fiscal transfers on a regular basis, ideally down to the school level. Publish average results and expenditure data at the regional level. Ensure that data are presented relative to standards, but also relative to capacity and disadvantage using some simple "value-added" concepts, and put more emphasis on trends than on levels at any particular time. The system should avoid reporting on a "passed" basis, or using standards for grade retention of students.

- Ensure that parent groups at the school level have the power to hold schools accountable by, for example, ensuring parents have a statutory majority on School Governing Councils (*Consejos Educativos Institucionales,* CEIs), and by requiring schools to report to parents on standards of achievement and resources received and used, according to simple, preset formats. Parents' Associations (*Asociaciónes de Padres de Familia,* APAFAs) should be equally accountable to the principals and the State. Parents should have a vote and voice in the promotion and selection of principals and teachers. This will act as an incentive for teachers to work towards satisfying the ultimate clients. However, as noted elsewhere, it is important that the clients be realistically informed about learning standards.

■ Encourage greater school-level autonomy for principals and parents, such as in the procurement of materials and the allocation of inputs, as long as there is both budgetary and results accountability. This can be encouraged by formula-based fiscal transfers to schools, as opposed to direct input provisioning of physical inputs.

■ Experiment more extensively with non-government administration of schools with public funding, similar to the *FyA* experience. Reduce the current ad hoc nature of these experiences by creating more standardized formats and contracts for management, and improving comparative evaluation of the experiences according to results and cost measurement. Disseminate the results.

■ UGELs should experiment with contracting out to service providers (see below). Schools should be explicitly asked to rate the services provided by UGELs or service providers, and this information should be used to modify provider behavior and to drive provider selection. The continuation and promotion of UGEL staff should be keyed to school ratings. Similarly, the process to promote and continue the employment of school personnel (principal and teachers) should be informed by parental rating of schools.

Support

Accountability pressure built around standards will lead to improved results only if one can assume that all actors have all the information and skills needed to come up to standard. This appears not to be the case in Peru. Thus, support is the third important leg on which qualitative improvement is needed.

■ Support is the area that will require the implementation work, and hence the most funding. Setting standards and accountability systems will require technical skill and creativity, as well as consensus building and dialogue ("political will"). But developing and using the support systems will, in addition, actually use up large amounts of scarce resources (particularly human resources), and is something that needs to be improved on over time.

■ Teachers need much more intensive support and "accompaniment" in how to teach to the learning standards. Generic and low-intensity cascade support is unlikely to work. Instead, week-by-week, or at least month-by-month accompaniment, based on measured results, is needed, at least for a few years. Experiments with massive and intensive training that instrumentally take teachers through a whole year's curriculum, and with specific, measurable goals (the standards), are needed. This should start with reading and with the first few grades, and can then be expanded to other skills and later grades.

■ Parent bodies need training in how to hold schools accountable for performance to standard and for budgetary and financial issues. This should include the development of reporting formats, and the training of parent bodies in how to use the formats to put pressure on schools. On the other hand, a clear distinction between a governance or accountability role, which is positive, and a daily management role for parents, which is likely to be negative, needs to be drawn, and both parents and principals need to be educated about this.

- School principals will need training in how to discharge their new accountability to parents and in how to perform to both outcome and process standards.

- Support will also be needed in helping both schools and UGELs make cogent use of performance information in driving decisions on personnel progression and pay. This will not be an easy task.

- UGELs and other intermediary institutions (such as DREs) are grossly under-equipped to provide support to schools on either pedagogical or administrative matters. At this point, they fulfill more of a control and harassment function, in the worst of cases, or a vertical reporting, or upward accountability, function, in the best of cases. Instead, UGEL personnel should be required and trained to support the accountability of schools to parents and community, realizing that schools are the front line of service provision, and are the quality "face" of the system. The regional and national governments, in turn, should be accountable to UGELs and schools; there should be some clear "downward" accountability. Importantly, the capacity of UGELs to support schools pedagogically needs to be strengthened. In most cases, this will take too long. In the meantime, experiments in outsourcing school support functions to NGOs or universities, in whole districts or even regions, can be developed. However, such support should be explicitly oriented at helping schools discharge accountability to standard; it should not be merely generic training on pedagogical theory and principles (as is all too common at present). Finally, this support should be rated for accountability purposes (see above).

- Overall budgetary support, in the form of increased expenditure (to pay for the resources needed to provide all of the above-mentioned support, but to pay for other improvements not discussed here, as well), should be developed, *pari passu*, once the various systems discussed here start to be developed and applied. It is unlikely that all these forms of accountability will produce results if the current levels of total budgetary support to education are maintained. For example, the levels of support and training needed to improve performance of teachers are likely to be massive. But expenditure support, if provided before proper forms of accountability are developed, will tend to flow along the current channels (expansion of numbers of teachers and schools). It would not tend to flow toward standards-based accountability support. While these channels were appropriate when the goal was to increase coverage, they are quite inappropriate when the goal is to improve quality; this, however, is what the systems are "trained" to do, and this is what the interest groups support.

- Fiscal support should be standardized (or formula-driven), as noted above. A simple way to do this is to make funding enrollment (or assistance) driven. Total funding (including personnel) from the national level to the regional level could be enrollment driven, with, perhaps, some differentiation for population density or poverty. For funding from the regional to school level, the formula could initially cover only non-personnel spending, and should provide more support to the poor by using simple targeting criteria such as the geographical location of the school.

■ Finally, and related to budgetary support, there is the issue of teacher costs. Since teacher costs consume the large majority of budgetary resources, the financing of teacher costs is the most important part of "support" to the education sector. Teacher costs have increased significantly in recent years. Yet, even prior to these increases, Peru had an oversupply of teachers. Yet, these teachers may not be of the quality and level of skills society needs. Increases in pay, if not tied to improved selection, incentives, and skills development, will not result in better teachers. It will result in further oversupply. At this point, instead of increases in pay, the focus should be on much more rigorous quality control at entry (selection through competition based on skills and knowledge, that is, standards-based selection and training), and improved selection over the career, including measures to encourage poor teachers to leave the profession.

Dogo

Había un perrito gordo y peludo llamado Dogo. La familia con quien vivía lo quería mucho.

Dogo era un perro obediente, cuidaba la casa, pero no comía toda su comida.

Un día salió de paseo con su amo Lucas y se perdió. Lucas se puso triste, pero felizmente Dogo apareció al rato. Lucas lo cargó y lo llevó a su casa.

Preguntas de comprensión (van en otra hoja)

1. ¿Cómo se llamaba el perro?
2. ¿Con quién vivía el perro?
3. ¿El perro comía toda su comida?

Classification and Frequency of Classroom Activities

Main Activity	Sub-activity	Observed Cases	Classification of Pedagogical Value
Teacher explaining a theme	Children listening attentively	12	Medium
Teacher working with groups of children	Teacher working with some children, others no specific activity	8	Medium
Transition activity	Teacher trying to organize class	7	Low
Teacher dictating to all children	Some children listening or copying, others reading on their own or distracted	6	Low
Classroom without specific activity	Chaos, impossible to determine predominant activity	6	Low
Teacher with no specific activity	Teacher talking causally, no goal	5	Low
Teacher dictating to all children	Almost all children copying or listening	4	Medium
Teacher working with groups of children	Teacher supervising group work	4	High
Children working on blackboard	Other children paying attention or copying	4	Medium
Classroom without specific activity	No teacher in classroom	3	Low
Classroom without specific activity	Teacher chatting with some students	3	Low
Teacher dictating to all children	Most children doing nothing and not paying attention	2	Low
Teacher explaining a theme	Most children doing nothing and not paying attention	2	Low
Teacher working with groups of children	Teacher working with some children, others no specific activity	2	Low

Children working on blackboard	Some children listening or copying, others reading on their own or distracted	2	Medium
Transition activity	Teacher distributing books and materials	2	Medium
Classroom without specific activity	Each child on his own without teacher involvement	2	Low
Teacher explaining a theme	Most children doing nothing and not paying attention	1	Low
Classroom without specific activity	Teacher writing on board without apparent goal	1	Low
Classroom with some specific child activity	Children reading for the others	1	Low
Classroom without specific activity	Teacher absent, children outside the classroom	1	Low
Classroom without specific activity	Dance practice outside the classroom	1	Low
Children working on blackboard	Most children doing nothing and not paying attention	0	Low
Children working on blackboard	Other	0	Medium
Children working together	Reading aloud together	0	High
Children working together	Taking turns reading	0	Medium
Children working together	Working on a common task with active teacher supervision	0	High
Classroom without specific activity	Children working on exam	0	Medium
Classroom without specific activity	Children working without teacher supervision	0	Low

Note: Two observations per classroom.

Bibliography

Abadzi, Helen. 2004. "Education for All or Just for the Smartest Poor?" *Prospects* 34:271–89.

ACTFL. Undated. "Standards for Foreign Language Teaching: Preparing for the 21st Century." Accessed at http://www.actfl.org/files/public/execsumm.pdf on June 11, 2005.

Alcázar, Lorena, and Nancy Cieza. 2002. "Hacia una mejor gestión de los centros educativos en el Perú: el caso de Fe y Alegría." Instituto Apoyo y CIES.

Alcázar, Lorena. 2004. "Agenda Nacional De Reformas Económicas En Perú: El Sector Educación." Group for the Analysis of Development. Lima, Peru Wordprocessed.

"Análisis del modelo de gestión institucional y pedagógica y lecciones para la educación pública." Group for the Analysis of Development. Lima, Peru.

Arregui, Patricia, Hugo Díaz, and Barbara Hunt. 1996. "Problemas, Perspectivas y Requerimientos de la Formación Magisterial en el Perú." Group for the Analysis of Development. Lima, Peru.

Arrisueño Fajardo, Gabriel. 2004. "Using Education To Heal Racism In Peru: Lessons From South Africa." Master's Thesis. The Maxwell School, Syracuse University. Processed.

Barr, R., C. Blachowicz, C. Katz, and B. Kaufman. 2002. "Reading Diagnosis for Teachers: An Instructional Approach (4th ed.)." Boston, MA: Allyn and Bacon.

Benavides, Martín. 2002. "Para Explicar Las Diferencias En El Rendimiento En Matemática De Cuarto Grado En El Perú Urbano: Análisis De Resultados A Partir De Un Modelo Básico." In Rodríguez, José, y Silvana Vargas, eds., *Análisis de los resultados y metodología de las pruebas CRECER 1998*. Documento De Trabajo No. 13. Programa MECEP. Ministerio de Educación.

Carnoy, Martin, and Michel Welmond. No date. "Do Teachers Get Paid Too Much? A Worldwide Comparison Of Teacher Pay." Wordprocessed draft.

Constance, Paul. 2003. *Escuela pública, gerencia privada*. Published in *BID América*, June.

Crouch, Luis. 2006. "Educación: Estándares, Apoyo y Rendición de Cuentas." In D. Cotlear, ed., *Un Nuevo Contrato Social Para El Perú: ¿Cómo lograr un país más educado, saludable, y solidario?* Washington, D.C.: The World Bank.

Crouch, Luis, and Tazeen Fasih. 2004. "Patterns in Educational Development." The World Bank. Processed.

Cruz, Gustavo, Giuliana Espinosa, Angélica Montané, Carlos Rodríguez. 2002. "Informe Técnico de la Consulta Nacional sobre Puntos de Corte para la Evaluación Nacional 2001." Ministerio De Educación, Unidad De Medición De La Calidad Educativa. Lima, Peru.

Cueto, Santiago and Walter Secada. 2001. "Mathematics Learning and Achievement in Quechua, Aymara and Spanish by Boys and Girls in Bilingual and Spanish Schools in Puno, Peru." Group for the Analysis of Development. Lima, Peru.

Cueto, Santiago, Cecilia Ramírez, and Juan León. 2003. "Eficacia escolar en escuelas polidocentes completas de Lima y Ayacucho." Group for the Analysis of Development. Lima, Peru. Processed.

Cueto, Santiago, Cecilia Ramírez, Juan León, and Oscar Pain. 2003. "Oportunidades de aprendizaje y rendimiento en matemática en una muestra de estudiantes de sexto grado de primaria de Lima." Documento de Trabajo 43. Group for the Analysis of Development. Lima, Peru.

Cueto, Santiago. 2003. "Factores Predictivos del Rendimiento Escolar, Deserción e Ingreso a Educación Secundaria en una Muestra de Estudiantes de Zonas Rurales del Perú." Group for the Analysis of Development. Lima, Peru.

Cummings, S. M. and Stella Tamayo. 1994. "Language and Education in Latin America: An Overview." *Human Resources Development and Operations Policy Working Papers (HROWP), No. 30.* Washington, D.C. The World Bank.

D'Emilio, Lucia. 1996. "Voices and Processes Toward Pluralism: Indigenous Education in Bolivia." Swedish International Development Cooperation Agency (SIDA). New Education Division Documents, No. 9. Stockholm, Sweden.

Danida. 2004. "Best practices for including indigenous peoples in sector programme support." A Toolkit. Draft.

De la Colina, María G., Richard Parker, Jan Hasbrouck, and Raphael Lara-Alecio. 2001. "Intensive Intervention in Reading Fluency for At-Risk Beginning Spanish Readers." *Bilingual Research Journal* 25(4):417–52.

Del Rosario, Mercedes and Nanda Warren. 2003. "Response to 'Whose Language Is it Anyway?' Historical Fetishism and the Construction of Expertise in Bolivian Language Planning." *Current Issues in Comparative Education* 5(2).

Department of Education. 2002. Revised National Curriculum Statement. Grades R-9 (Schools). Pretoria, South Africa. Sourced at http://education.pwv.gov.za/DoE_Sites/Curriculum/Final%20curriculum/policy/English/Eng%20Home%20Language%20Fin.pdf on 20 February 2005.

Díaz, Hugo, and Jaime Saavedra. 2000. "La Carrera del Maestro en el Perú: Factores Institucionales, Incentivos Económicos, y Desempeño." Lima, Perú. GRADE. Documento de Trabajo No. 32.

Dutcher, Nadine, with the collaboration of G. Richard Tucker. 1997. "The Use of First and Second Languages in Education. A Review of International Experience." Pacific Islands Discussion Paper Series. No. 1. The World Bank. Washington D.C.

Equipo de Análisis de la Unidad de Medición de la Calidad Educativa. 2004. "Factores Aso-
ciados Al Rendimiento Estudiantil." Unidad de Medición de la Calidad Educativa.
Ministerio de Educación. Lima, Peru. Processed.

Equipo de Orientación Educativa de Marbella. 2003. "Evaluación de la velocidad lectora
oral y Análisis de la correlación de esta variable con la nota global de junio." Conse-
jería de Educación y Ciencia. Junta de Andalucía.

Equipo Pedagógico Nacional de FyA. 2003. Propuesta pedagógica. Lima, Peru.

Espinosa, Giuliana and Alberto Torreblanca. 2003. "Resultados de las Pruebas de Comunicación y Matemática de la Evaluación Nacional del Rendimiento Estudiantil 2001."
Ministerio de Educación, Unidad de Medición de la Calidad Educativa. Lima, Peru.
Sourced at http://www.minedu.gob.pe/umc/2003/pdfs_nac/result_pruebas_commat.
pdf on 20 February 2005.

FyA. 2003. FyA: Movimiento de Educación Popular Integral y Promoción Social. Presentation available at www.feyalegria.org.

Fiszbein, Ariel, editor. 2005. "Citizens, Politicians, and Providers: The Latin American
Experience with Service Delivery Reform." The World Bank, Washington, D.C.

Foro del Acuerdo Nacional. 2004. Pacto Social De Compromisos Recíprocos Por La
Educación 2004–2006. Sourced at http://www.acuerdonacional.gob.pe/Pactos/
PactoSocialdeEducaci%F3n.pdf on July 2, 2004.

Francke, Pedro. 2004. "Educación pública, salud y descentralización." Universidad Pontificia Católica del Peru. Palestra Web-Site. Sourced at http://palestra.pucp.edu.pe/?id=38
on July 23, 2004.

Galindo, Claudia. 2002. "El Currículo Implementado Como Indicador Del Proceso Educativo." In José Rodríguez and Silvana Vargas, eds., *Análisis de los resultados y metodología
de las pruebas CRECER 1998*. Documento De Trabajo No. 13. Programa MECEP. Ministerio de Educación.

Grimaldo Vásquez, Rengifo. 2003. "La Enseñanza Es Estar Contento: Educación y Afirma-
ción Cultural Andina." Proyecto Andino de Tecnologías Campesinas (PRATEC).
Lima, Peru. Processed.

Guzmán, Ingrid, Leonel Penacho and Alicia Gonzáles. 2002. "Sistematización en Torno a
la Capacitación Docente en EBI Desarrollada por la DINEBI." Lima, Peru. Processed.

Herrera, S. and G. Pang, 2004. "Efficiency of public spending in developing countries: and
efficiency frontier approach." A World Bank Economic Policy Paper. Washington, D.C.

Hoffman, J. V., P. D. Pearson, S. N. Beretvas, and M. Sailors. 2003. "The Business Trust:
Learning for Living Project: Year 3 Progress Report." The READ Trust. Johannes-
burg. Sourced at http://www.read.org.za/news/READ%20Final%202003.pdf on 19
February 2005.

Hornberger, Nancy, and Serafín Coronel-Molina. 2004. "Quechua language shift, main-
tenance, and revitalization in the Andes: the case for language planning." *International
Journal of the Sociology of Language* 167:9–67.

Hornberger, Nancy. 2000. "Bilingual Education Policy and Practice in the Andes: Ideolog-
ical Paradox and Intercultural Possibility." *Anthropology and Education Quarterly*
31(2).

Hunt, Barbara. 2001. "Peruvian Primary Education: Improvement Still Needed." Prepared
for delivery at the meeting of the Latin American Studies Association, Washington,
D.C., September 6–8. Processed.

Instituto Superior Pedagógico Público Loreto. 1992. "Diseño Curricular de Formación Docente en Educación Intercultural Bilingüe para la Amazonía Peruana." Iquitos, Peru.

"Investments, Incentives and Institutions." Report of the Task Force on Education and Gender Equality. New York.

Rivero, José. 2002. "Magisterio, Educación y Sociedad en el Perú." Ministerio de Educación y UNESCO. Lima, Peru.

Rivero, José. 2004. "Políticas educativas y exclusión: sus límites y complejidad." Sourced at http://palestra.pucp.edu.pe/?id=48, on July 23, 2004.

Jung, Ingrid and Luis Enrique López. 1989. "Sistematización del Proyecto Experimental de Educación Bilingüe Puno (PEEB-P), 1977–1988." GTZ. Lima, Perú. Second edition.

Kuper, Wolfgang. 1988. "Interculturalidad y Reforma Educativa en Tres Países Andinos." Pueblos Indígenas y Educación. Nos. 45–46. Abya Yala. GTZ. Quito, Ecuador.

Lazcano, Josefa. 2003. "FyA. Las claves de una experiencia exitosa". Prepared for a seminar on "Experiencias exitosas de Capital Social" at the International Seminar on Social Capital, Ethics, and Development: The Challenges of Democratic Governance, Caracas, June 25–26.

López, Luis Enrique. 2002. "A ver, a ver . . . ¿Quién quiere salir a la pizarra? ¿Jumasti? Jupasti?" Programa MECEP. Documento de Trabajo No. 15. Ministerio de Educación. Lima, Peru.

Hernani Limarino, Werner. 2004. "Are teachers well paid in LAC? Relative wage and structure of returns of teachers in LAC." Processed.

Luykx, Aurolyn. 2004. "The future of Quechua and the Quechua of the future: language ideologies and language planning in Bolivia." *International Journal of the Sociology of Language* 167:147–58.

Martiniello, María. 2001. "Fe y Alegría: Where Community is the Choice." Graduate School of Education, Harvard University.

McMeekin, R. W., Marcela Latorre, and Francisca Zeledón. 2001. "Instituciones dentro de las organizaciones escolares." Processed.

Mealla, Eloy. "ONGs y Administración Pública: la experiencia de Fe y Alegría." *Revista Colecciones* VII(11). Buenos Aires.

Ministerio de Educación de Chile. Undated. "Desempeños a Lograr en Escritura, Lectura, y Matemáticas, 2ndo Nivel de Transición, Nivel Básico 1, Nivel Básico 2." Santiago, Chile. Sourced at http://biblioteca.mineduc.cl/documento/desempenos-ultimo3.pdf on 20 February 2005.

Ministerio de Educación del Perú (MINEDU). 2000. "Estructura Curricular Básica de Educación Primaria de Menores." Documento elaborado por la Dirección Nacional de Educación Inicial y Primaria.

———. 2001. "Los Desafios de la Diversidad." DINEIP—UNEBI. FORTE PE. Lima, Peru.

———. 2004. "Contribución al Desarrollo de la Educación en Areas Rurales: Sistematización de la Experiencia en Cuatro Ámbitos Seleccionados." Oficina de Coordinación para el desarrollo Educativo Rural. Lima, Peru.

Ministerio de Educación del Perú/Dirección de Educación Inicial y Primaria. 2000. "Programa Curricular de Educación Primaria de Menores. (Primer y segundo grados) Estructura Curricular Básica de Educación Primaria de Menores." Lima, Peru. Accessed at http://www.minedu.gob.pe/gestion_pedagogica/dir_edu_inicial_primaria/2003/dir.php?obj=curriculo2003.htm, on 20 February 2005.

Montero, Carmen (coordinadora). 2001. "La Escuela Rural: Modalidades y Prioridades de Intervención." Ministerio de Educación. Lima, Peru.

Montero, Carmen, Patricia Ames, Zoila Cabrera, Andrés Chirinos, Mariella Fernández Dávila, and Eduardo León. 2002. "Propuesta metodológica para el mejoramiento de la enseñanza y el aprendizaje en el aula rural multigrado." Documento de Trabajo No. 18. Programa MECEP. Ministerio de Educación.

Navarro, Juan Carlos. 2002. "Y sin embargo se mueve: Educación de financiamiento público y gestión privada en el Perú." In Lawrence Wolf, Pablo González, and Juan Carlos Navarro, *Educación privada y política pública en América Latina*. Santiago: PREAL/BID.

Ndoye, Mamadou. 2003. "Bilingualism, language policies, and educational strategies in Africa." *IIEP Newsletter* (July-September).

Organisation for Economic Cooperation and Development (OECD). 2005. Worksheet on teacher salaries sourced on May 29, 2005, at http://www.oecd.org/dataoecd/61/34/33671263.xls.

Organisation for Economic Cooperation and Development (OECD) and Unesco Institute of Statistics (UIS). 2003. "Literacy Skills for the World of Tomorrow: Further Results from PISA 2000." Paris: OECD.

Oliart, Patricia. 2002. "Qué Podemos Aprender de las Escuelas Rurales: Reflexiones Acerca de los Dilemas de la Escuela Rural en la Sierra Peruana." *Escuelas que Aprenden y se Desarrollan*. Universidad Peruana Cayetano Heredia. Lima, Peru.

Orr Easthouse, Linda. 2004. "Literacy: Freedom depends on who holds the tools." Word-processed. Wycliffe Canada.

Passolunghi, C. M, C. Cornoldi and S. de Libero. 1999. "Working memory and intrusions of irrelevant information in a group of specific problem solvers." *Memory and Cognition* 27(5):779–90.

Pérez Villar, José. 1996. "¿Cómo lee mi paciente?: Contribución a la metodología del examen directo en psiquiatría de niños." *Revista Cubana de Pediatría* 68(3).

Ponencia presentada para el Seminario sobre Escuela Rural Andina. Tarea. Cusco, Peru.

Pontificia Universidad Católica del Perú. 1995. "Una Propuesta Andina de Profesionalización Docente." CRAM Urubamba. CISE. Lima, Peru.

PREAL (Programa de Promoción Educativa en América Latina y el Caribe). 2003. "Informe de Progreso Educativo–Perú."

———. 2004. "Mexico: Programa Atención Educativa a Población Indígena (PAEPI)." Serie "Buenas Prácticas." Sourced at http://www.preal.org/Biblioteca.asp?Id_Carpeta=118&Camino=80|Buenas%20Prácticas/104|Banco%20de%20Datos%20Buenas%20Prácticas%20de%20Política%20Educacional%20y%20Reforma%20Educativa/106 Experiencias%20registradas%20según%20país/118|México accessed on Feb 06, 2007.

Public Schools of North Carolina. 2003. "English Language Development: Standard Course of Study and Grade Level Competencies." Department of Public Instruction, Raleigh, North Carolina, USA.

Raczynski, Dagmar and Gonzalo Muñoz. 2005. "Effective Schools in Poverty Areas in Chile. Keys And Challenges." Asesorías para el Desarrollo, Santiago, Chile. Processed.

Reisberg, D. 2001. *Cognition: Exploring the Science of the Mind*. Second edition. New York: Norton.

Red EBI Perú. 1999. "Congreso Nacional De Educación Intercultural Bilingüe 1998." In *Educación Bilingüe Intercultural: Experiencias y Propuestas*. GTZ. Lima, Perú.

Reimers, Fernando. 1993. "FyA: una innovación educativa para proporcionar educación básica con calidad y equidad." Harvard Institute for International Development. Processed.

Rivero, José. 2004. "Políticas Regionales Andinas para el Desarrollo de la Escuela Rural." Lima, Peru. Processed.

Rodas, Antonio. 1999. "Experiencia Pedagógica del Proyecto de Educación Bilingüe Intercultural de Andahuylas Chincheros-PEBIACH." In "Educación Bilingüe Intercultural: Experiencias y Propuestas. GTZ." Lima, Peru.

Rodríguez, José. 2004. "Importancia del gasto público de calidad en la educación." Universidad Pontificia Católica del Perú. Palestra website. Accessed at http://palestra.pucp. edu.pe/?id=25 on July 23, 2004.

Romero, Leonor y Nelly Cáceres. 2001. "Fe y Alegría: Una alternativa educativa de calidad para los empobrecidos." Universidad Peruana Cayetano Heredia, Facultad de Educación.

Sakellariou, Chris. 2004. "The Indigenous/Non-Indigenous Early Test Score Gap in Bolivia, Perú and México." Applied Economics. School of Humanities and Social Science. Nanyang Technological University. Singapore. Processed.

Shaywitz, Sally. 2003. *Overcoming Dyslexia.* New York: Alfred Knopf.

Ramírez, Eliana. 2003. "Balance de las Experiencias de Educación Rural en el Perú."

Saavedra, J., and E. Maruyama, 1999. "Los retornos a la educación y a la experiencia en el Perú: 1985–1997." Grupo de Análisis para el Desarrollo, GRADE, Lima, Peru.

Swope, John y Marcela Latorre. 1998. *Comunidades Educativas Donde Termina el Asfalto, Escuelas Fe y Alegría en América Latina.* Santiago, Chile: Centro de Investigación y Desarrollo de la Educación.

Trapnell, Lucy and Eloy Neira. 2004. "Situación de la Educación Intercultural Bilingüe en el Perú." Consultancy for the World Bank. Working document.

Trapnell, Lucy and others. 2004. "Balance y Perspectivas de la EIB en el Perú." Conclusiones presentadas por la delegación peruana en el Seminario Internacional Balance y Perspectivas de la EIB en América Latina in Cochabamba, Bolivia.

Tucker, G. Richard. 1999. "A Global Perspective on Bilingualism and Bilingual Education." Center for Applied Linguistics. August. Accessed at http://www.cal.org/resources/digest/ digestglobal.html on March 13, 2005.

Uccelli, Francesca. 1999. "Familias Campesinas, Educación y Democracia en el Sur Andino." Instituto de Estudios Peruanos (IEP). Documento de Trabajo. Lima, Peru.

Universidad Peruana Cayetano Heredia, Facultad de Educación. 2001. Primer Seminario Internacional Investigación para una mejor educación. Escuelas que aprenden y se desarrollan. Lima. Processed.

Vega, Juan Fernando. 2004. "La autoridad de los padres de familia como base de la política educativa." Sourced at http://www.palestra.pucp.edu.pe/index.php?id=24 on February 06, 2004.

Vigil, Nila. 2004. "Pueblos Indígenas y Escritura." Accessed at http://www.aulaintercultural. org/IMG/pdf/indigenas_escritura.pdf on March 20, 2005.

Webb, Richard, and Sofía Valencia. 2006. "Los Recursos Humanos en La Salud y La Educación Públicas del Perú." In D. Cotlear, ed., *Un Nuevo Contrato Social Para El Perú: ¿Cómo lograr un país más educado, saludable, y solidario?* Washington D.C.: The World Bank.

Wolf, Lawrence, Pablo González, and Juan Carlos Navarro. 2002. *Educación privada y política pública en América Latina.* Santiago: PREAL/BID.

World Bank. 2001. "Peruvian Education at a Crossroads: Challenges and Opportunities for the 21st Century." A World Bank Country Report, No. 22357. Washington, D.C.

———. 2003. *Making Services Work for Poor People. World Development Report 2004.* World Bank. Washington, D.C.

———. 2004. "Education in Indonesia: Managing the Transition to Decentralization." Human Development Sector Reports, East Asia and Pacific Region. Report No. 29506.

———. undated. "Implications for Further Efficiency Analysis." Washington D.C. Processed.

Zavala, Virginia. 2002. "Desencuentros con la Escritura: Escuela y Comunidad en los Andes Peruanos." Red para el Desarrollo de las Ciencias Sociales en el Perú. Lima, Peru.

Zúñiga, Madeleine, Liliana Sánchez, and Daniela Zacharías. 2002. "Demanda y Necesidad De Educación Bilingüe: Lenguas Indígenas y Castellano en el Sur Andino." German Agency for Technical Cooperation, KFW. Ministerio de Educación. Lima, Peru.

Eco-Audit

Environmental Benefits Statement

The World Bank is committed to preserving Endangered Forests and natural resources. We print World Bank Working Papers and Country Studies on 100 percent postconsumer recycled paper, processed chlorine free. The World Bank has formally agreed to follow the recommended standards for paper usage set by Green Press Initiative—a nonprofit program supporting publishers in using fiber that is not sourced from Endangered Forests. For more information, visit www.greenpressinitiative.org.

In 2006, the printing of these books on recycled paper saved the following:

Trees*	Solid Waste	Water	Net Greenhouse Gases	Total Energy
203	9,544	73,944	17,498	141 mil.
'40" in height and 6-8" in diameter	Pounds	Gallons	Pounds CO$_2$ Equivalent	BTUs

green press
INITIATIVE